HELD IN TRUST

HELD IN TRUST

THE NATIONAL TRUST FOR SCOTLAND

IAIN CRAWFORD

A CHANNEL FOUR / SCOTTISH TELEVISION BOOK

MAINSTREAM
PUBLISHING

First published in the United Kingdom by
Mainstream Publishing in conjunction with the Scottish Television
documentary series, *Held in Trust*.

MAINSTREAM PUBLISHING COMPANY (EDINBURGH), LTD.
7 Albany Street
Edinburgh EH1 3UG

British Library Cataloguing in Publication Data

Held in trust: the National Trust for Scotland.
1. National Trust for Scotland
I. Title
363.6'9'06041   DA873

ISBN 0-906391-79-2

Typeset in 12 point Van Dijke by Mainstream Publishing.
Printed by Collins, Glasgow, Great Britain.

CONTENTS

ACKNOWLEDGEMENTS

OBVIOUSLY, in a book like this many people have made important contributions to its content, although only I am responsible for the manner of its presentation. I should like to thank the on-site representatives of the National Trust for Scotland who made me welcome at their properties, often out of season, particularly Dr John and Mrs Margaret Lorne Campbell of Canna, Mr Michael Tebbutt of Culzean, Mr Stewart Thomson of Fair Isle, Mr Hew Lorimer of Kellie Castle, Miss Chrissie McGillivray of Burg, Mrs Nancy Walter of Ecclefechan and Mr Lea MacNally of Torridon. I am also very grateful to Mrs Judy Aitken at the Trust's headquarters in Charlotte Square who was invariably helpful in finding information material relating to the properties and there is a huge debt of gratitude owed to the many people who have written the pamphlets and booklets about the Trust's properties which provide the prime sources. Sincere thanks are due to Scottish Television who financed a year of travel around Scotland while I researched the properties of the National Trust for the documentary series *Held In Trust* intended for transmission on Scottish Television and Channel Four; also to Russell Galbraith, Assistant Controller of Programmes, who commissioned me to write the series on which this book is based. Many thanks are also due to the series presenter Diana Rigg, and the Programme Director, Alan Macmillan, for their valuable advice and encouragement; and to Sheena McDonald for her assistance in the preparation of the television script material. My thanks are also due to June Homer, who helped with the research and some 6,000 miles of travel involved and to Kathy Hay, who typed some of the manuscript.

For my son, Michael, in happy recall of the many voyages we have made together in many countries, in love and friendship.

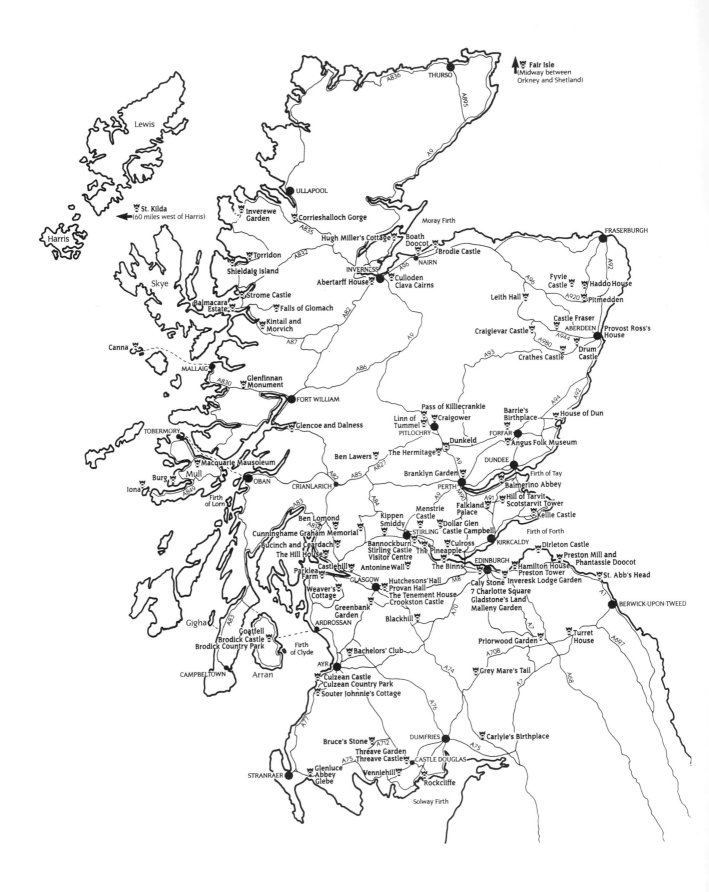

1

THE TRUST

CONSERVATION is, relatively speaking, a new idea. Down the ages it has been evident in some agricultural practices like irrigation, terracing and replanting of depleted long-term resources like forestry but its application was strictly pragmatic. Primitive man represented no threat to his environment; his numbers were small, his technology simple and his destructive impact on the world around him was minimal. If he exhausted the resources of one place he just moved on.

As the world population increased, practical conservation crept in. Animals protected by religious taboos, sacred forest groves and mountains, hunting lands reserved for nobles and royalty were early forms. The development of settled communities and the need for static agricultural techniques made for scientific advancement in farming, forestry and land use but the impetus came from need rather than will.

The modern conservation movement began in America in the first part of the nineteenth century as a result of the enormous and literally devastating changes in the environment seen by just one generation — the virtual elimination of the bison and other indigenous animals and the extinction of whole areas of native vegetation. The idea of National Parks was proposed as early as 1832 by American writer and painter, George Catlin, who was supported by the botanist, William Bartram, and the famous ornithologist and bird painter, John James Audubon. The writers Ralph Waldo Emerson and Henry Thoreau joined the campaign and in the 1860s the first textbook on conservation was published, *Man and Nature* by George Perkins Marsh, an American diplomat and scholar of extraordinary talents (he was fluent in 20 languages by the age of 30!). This formidably literate campaign combined with the strong passion for the outdoor life which was (and still is) part of the American character, resulted in the opening of the world's first

National Park in the Yosemite Valley in California in 1864, followed eight years later by the designation by the US Congress of Yellowstone Park in Wyoming as a National Park.

Archaeology on the other hand has a longer and decidedly more murky past. The first 'archaeologists' — in the sense that they took an interest in artifacts from the past — were Sumerian, Hittite and Egyptian grave-robbers who, knowing that people of importance were buried under the practice of these cultures with objects precious to them in life, broke into tombs to steal gold, jewels and objects of value.

The word 'archaeology' is constructed from two Greek words, *archaia* and *logos* — 'ancient objects' and 'theory' or 'science' — and therefore means the study of the science of the past — a branch of historical study based on the accidentally surviving remnants of past human activities and creations. Until the eighteenth century, it meant virtually 'treasure hunting'. As the scholars of the Renaissance period in the fifteenth and sixteenth centuries began to look back admiringly at the splendours of Greece and Rome, wealthy people, popes, cardinals and noblemen wished to acquire objects associated with these periods as decorations for their splendid palaces and villas. Indiscriminate excavation was encouraged and paid for, probably doing more damage to the relics of past civilisations than the grave robbers ever had. However, in some cases, at least it meant that some of the objects were preserved, albeit frequently without any precise historical or geographical provenance, and not broken up.

True archaeology, as we know it today, which is concerned with the preservation and illumination of the past and occupies itself not only with beautiful and precious things, really began in the eighteenth century with the excavation of the sites of the lava-drowned cities of Pompeii and Herculaneum on the Gulf of Naples. At first it was not much more than treasure-hunting by predatory Austrian and French rulers but, in the unique circumstances of the Vesuvius eruptions which had buried both cities, there was so much to be found that in the course of the many years of excavations proper scholarly and respectful methods came to be used.

So, modern conservation and archaeology are both more concerned with historical, aesthetic and preservation reasons than agricultural pragmatism and loot. The treasures held in trust for us by the National Trust for Scotland embrace the disciplines of conservation and archaeological and historical interest in a unique way. The Trust's main obligation is to preserve the landscape, wildlife, buildings, gardens, historic sites and islands of Scotland for the enjoyment of us all. To do that it has to be not only a custodian of some of the most beautiful and fascinating places in the country but it must be innovative and enterprising as well, not just a watchdog but a teacher, a contributor to the public good; active, not passive, in the preservation of what is best and most interesting

Kintail: Ross and Cromarty.

in the heritage of Scotland. In the 55 years of its existence, it has filled its remit
with passion, elegance and conviction.

The National Trust for Scotland was founded in 1931, derivative in many
ways from the National Trust in England which was established in 1895, itself a
development of the Commons Preservation Society set up in 1865 to defend the
right of the public to have access to common land and open spaces in general for
recreation. The word 'Trust' most probably emanated from America (which now
has such a profound *mis*trust of the word that it has 'Anti-Trust' laws!) because
the concern of Americans with conservation had led in 1891 to the incorporation of
the Trustees of Public Reservations in Massachussetts.

The initiative in Scotland came from the Association for the Preservation of

11

Rural Scotland who, like the Commons Preservation Society in London, was prevented by statute from acquiring land or buildings. Sir Iain Colquhoun of Luss, the Chairman, strongly supported by Sir John Stirling Maxwell of Pollock wanted to change all this and on 1 May 1931 The National Trust for Scotland for Places of Historical Interest or Natural Beauty was born. It was constituted as an independent body capable of working with statutory authorities and with the power to hold land, buildings and chattels 'for the benefit of the nation'. In 1935 the passing of the National Trust for Scotland Act made the Trust a statutory body, enabling the Council to declare Trust lands and buildings inalienable — to be held by the Trust in perpetuity, a holding which can be broken only by Parliamentary legislation.

Today, the National Trust for Scotland has in its care some one hundred properties, throughout the length and breadth of the land from the Solway Firth to the remote Fair Isle, half way between Orkney and Shetland; from St Kilda far out in the Western Ocean to Provost Ross's House, overlooking the oil-rich harbour of Aberdeen on the North Sea. 100,000 acres of wild country, mountains, islands and moorland, historical sites such as the battlefields of Bannockburn and Culloden, the Pass of Killiecrankie and the site of the raising of the standard in the 1745 Rising at Glenfinnan; great houses and castles, humble houses and workshops and hundreds of acres of glorious gardens come within its care.

But the Trust is not just about artifacts and places, no matter how splendid many of these may be. Ultimately it is about people. How they lived as well as where they lived in the past.

Its remit covers not only important parts of our history but what the developments arising from it mean to us now. Its concern embraces what is worth preserving from peaks and islands to beautiful gardens and great castles. This heritage is not just a vast museum — although it is that too. It is something to be shared and enjoyed, all these wonderful places and eye-catching buildings, whether your taste is for wilderness or Georgian elegance, history on the spot or activities like walking the great hills or helping to preserve an isolated and threatened community. There is a future as well as a past, something that has to be worked for. Without the voluntary workers who give their time and labour and skill and without the Trust raising some of its own revenue by subscriptions and such activities as selling plants from its gardens and running seventeen shops, it could not function as it does.

What the National Trust for Scotland holds for us is partly a realisation of who we are and how we came to be that way. Its work makes the heritage of the past a part of our present and a series of treasures available to everyone a part of the future.

2

HOW THE TRUST WORKS

THE MOST northerly property of the National Trust for Scotland, Fair Isle, lies on the frontier between the Atlantic and the North Sea; the most westerly, St Kilda, 110 miles out in the Atlantic off the Scottish mainland and 50 miles beyond the Outer Hebrides.

St Kilda was abandoned as an anachronism of living in the 1930s after a more or less continuous inhabitance of more than 3,000 years. How or why late Neolithic men should ever have settled in this remote, wind and sea-battered island group is still a mystery, although more books have been written about St Kilda than any comparable group of islands in the British Isles. There are archaeological remains on the island but they have never been properly excavated. The inhabitants lived very largely off seabirds and their eggs — the islands are one of the principal breeding places for gannets, fulmars and puffins in Europe and have their own particular species of wren, a furry field mouse and a breed of primitive sheep not found elsewhere — but regular contact with the outside world after early tourists and ornithologists discovered St Kilda early in the nineteenth century bred discontent, disease and finally abandonment.

One of the more notable inhabitants was a bad-tempered lady who was married to a secretly Jacobite judge in Edinburgh. She was exiled to St Kilda when she threatened to expose her husband's political affiliations in the period between the 1715 and 1745 rebellions. Lord Grange, brother to the Earl of Mar who led the 1715 rebellion had his wife kidnapped and removed eventually to Hirta, one of the St Kilda group, where she was pitilessly isolated in a community whose inhabitants spoke nothing but Gaelic and who did not understand what a Jacobite was.

Incidentally, there never was a Saint Kilda. The name is thought to be due to a faulty transliteration of Skildar or Skaldir, Norse words meaning a shield, in a

St Kilda: The Village.

seventeenth century set of Dutch sailing directions. The St Kilda islands belonged to the Macleods who in 1934 sold them to the Earl of Dumfries, later to become the fifth Marquess of Bute. After the Marquess's death in 1956, the islands were bequeathed to the National Trust for Scotland, who, not without some soul-searching, decided to accept the bequest in 1957. The Trust leased the group to the Nature Conservancy Council who, with the Trust's agreement, leased part of Hirta, the largest island, to the Ministry of Defence for use as a missile-tracking station.

This rather strange arrangement has worked very well. Although there is little chance of the islands being repopulated, co-operation between the Army and voluntary labour teams from the Trust has enabled some of the cottages of the original village to be restored to provide basic accommodation for volunteers and other visitors and has allowed further restoration work to be carried out. This work provides a base from which other researches can be mounted, so that the mysteries surrounding St Kilda may yet be solved.

On Fair Isle the tale is a much happier one. This island, lying 24 miles south-west of Sumburgh Head in Shetland, is the Frideray of the Norse sagas. Its three square miles of turf-carpeted soaring sea-cliffs, scattered with small, neat, mostly white-painted cottages, with sheep and cattle dotted in the low ground between the headlands and the hills, have an air of prosperity which, despite the island's remoteness, is not an illusion.

It lies on one of the principal bird migration tracks. More than 300 different species of bird migrants have been recorded there since 1948 — 190 of them regular visitors — together with some rare ones, seldom seen anywhere else in the British Isles. There was once a regular steamer service to Fair Isle, which has always enjoyed a reputation for its intricately patterned knitwear, and Victorian travellers were the first to observe the variety and density of the island's bird life. During the last war, two Scots in a German prisoner-of-war camp, both keen ornithologists, decided to buy the island and create a bird observatory there. In 1948, George Waterston and Ian Pitman bought Fair Isle and set up the first bird observatory in the huts of a wartime naval outpost.

By 1954, although the bird-watching activity was as lively as ever, George Waterston could see that the island needed help. The population was declining and he realised he might soon be left with an empty island on his hands, and without people on the island it would be difficult to continue and maintain the bird-watching facilities. He approached the National Trust for Scotland and arranged to sell the island to them. So the Trust became the landlord, a major responsibility, taking on the burden not only of being the guardian of the island's wildlife and amenities but also the onus of keeping people on Fair Isle. Depopulation was a very real threat. Many of the crofts were in poor condition and people were talking about leaving. Many had already left. Although bird-watchers made up an enthusiastic band of visitors, accommodation for them in the old naval huts by the North Haven was elementary and access to the island was difficult.

With the help of other bodies like the Scottish Office, The Zetland County Council, the Highlands and Islands Development Board, private charitable trusts and the co-operation of the Fair Isle Bird Observatory Trust, all that has been changed. The women of Fair Isle, knitting garments with their distinctive and unique patterns, have found markets with such a demand that there is an international waiting list for genuine Fair Isle knitwear. International voluntary labour brought in by the Trust has helped to modernise the croft houses. There is now an airstrip and regular Loganair services from Shetland supplement the boat service provided by *The Good Shepherd*, the island's own mail boat. The Bird Observatory now has a new building, opened in 1969 a little farther up the hill from North Haven, and specially designed as a hostel for visitors with room for 24 guests — probably the best one of its kind in the British Isles.

Fair Isle has a unique reputation for bird-watching. It is on the regular migration route for warblers, thrushes and finches, geese from Iceland and Spitzbergen, all kinds of birds coming out of Scandinavia, Iceland, Greenland, North America and Siberia. One day in 1969 there were an estimated 65,000 redwings on the island and in general Fair Isle observers have added more birds to the British list than any other location in the British Isles. A programme of netting birds, ringing them and releasing them has produced valuable ornithological information. Some 10,000 birds a year are ringed, more than at anywhere else in Britain. An Arctic Skua ringed on Fair Isle was found on the coast of Brazil; a Rustic Bunting in the Greek Islands; a Bar-Tailed Godwit (what else?) in Siberia; a Snow Bunting in the Canadian Arctic.

There are breeding colonies of Great and Arctic Skuas — which, as in St Kilda, have been accused of attacking humans and sheep in the breeding season — and all kinds of gulls, puffins, shags and eider ducks. Fair Isle has a reputation for rare birds too. There are a few of them every season — a Sandhill Crane from Canada, a Tennessee Warbler from the United States or a Siberian Rubythroat from Russia's Arctic coast.

Fair Isle is a wonderful place in which to watch birds. The steep cliffs and narrow gorges of the craggy, indented coastline make observation easy. The sheep-cropped carpet of grass and heather on top and the myriad pattern of the wild flowers which mottle the cliffs in a *pointilliste* shimmer of pink, white, blue and yellow provide other delights for the eye against the vast, empty background of the sea, with Orkney to the south and Foula and Shetland to the north, pale mauve smudges on the horizon.

But not everyone goes to Fair Isle to watch birds. The island is wild and lovely; there are Neolithic remains and magnificent cliff and hill walks, as well as strange stones marked with fire in a field behind Setter croft. Although it caters primarily for bird-watchers, the Bird Observatory welcomes any guests because it operates as a non-profitmaking organisation solely on its earned income as a hostel as well as a field-work centre for ornithology. Every night after supper there is a bird count when everyone out and about the island during the day reports on the birds they have seen for the daily log. Even if you can hardly tell a sparrow from a condor it is hard not to join in.

As well as birds, Fair Isle has a fair number of feral cats and the most variegated collection of rabbits I have ever seen — there are brown rabbits, black rabbits, white rabbits, peach-coloured rabbits, rabbits marked like Siamese cats, black and white, brown and white, long-furred, short-furred, some of them as big as hares. They take quite a toll of the islanders' gardens and crops and the Fair Islanders try to keep the numbers down by shooting. But they are difficult to trap because of the cliffs. 'They hide in there and you can't get at them,' Stewart Thomson told me, 'and they know it!'

Fair Isle.
Canna.

Tourism — bird-watchers and others — has become part of the economy of Fair Isle for the seventy inhabitants. In 1984 there was even a delegation from Spain, *La Armada del Mar Oceano*, dressed in sixteenth-century Spanish costume. They came, rather belatedly, to thank the islanders for their hospitality to two hundred of their ancestors, when *El Gran Grifon*, flagship of one of the transport sections of the Spanish Armada, was driven ashore into Stromhellier, a sea gully or geo in the south-east of the island in 1588. As the wrecked Spaniards outnumbered the islanders by at least two to one, the 'hospitality' may have been as much politic as warm-hearted. It is also said that, as an aftermath to that visit the elaborate patterns of Fair Isle knitwear were copied from the colourful uniforms of the Armada sailors.

Likely enough they had little idea of what brought *El Gran Grifon* into their angry seas but the islanders certainly have plenty of experience in welcoming shipwrecked mariners. There are more than forty wrecks round the rugged coast of the island — the earliest a Viking longship — and when the weather is fine, Fair Isle is a fascinating place for underwater exploration.

Stewart Thomson, son of the National Trust for Scotland's representative on the island, who is a diver, says there are still a few cannon from the Spanish ship under the sea off Fair Isle — one fine bronze specimen is in Lerwick Museum —and lots of cannon balls but no treasure. Any valuables would have been in the after section of the vessel and the poop broke off in the storm and was carried out to sea and sank in deeper water.

Today, the small community of Fair Isle is vibrant and alive. The electricity supply from diesel generators is supplemented by an aerogenerator — the first commercial experiment of its kind in the British Isles. There is work knitting and fishing and crofting; there is that special feeling of people working together, belonging to one very particular unit. The help-your-neighbour feeling is very strong on Fair Isle and there is a lot of community activity. When the islanders — and any visitors who are on the island — get together every fortnight for a dance at the Hall in the southern half of the island, the band is local — Stewart Thomson senior, the Trust's man on Fair Isle, his son Ewen Thomson and his grandson, Stewart Thomson! There is even an island newspaper, *Fair Isle Times*, printed on the island 40 times a year.

Everything about the National Trust for Scotland is implicit on this island —its concern with the environment, the wildlife, the preservation and restoration of its buildings and amenities, its duties as a landlord which do not fall into these categories and, above all, its enthusiasm for improving the quality of life and being deeply involved in the happiness and well-being of the people who live on Fair Isle as well as its visitors.

The priorities are rather different 250 miles to the south-west in Glen Coe, the great rock gash which runs from the edge of Rannoch Moor to the waters of the sea-fed Loch Leven. This is one of the most evocative place names of Scotland; it has the stain of blood and treachery on it because it was here that one hundred and twenty men of the Earl of Argyll's Regiment of Foot commanded by Captain Robert Campbell of Glenlyon, having accepted the traditional Highland hospitality of MacIain and the Macdonalds of Glen Coe, rose from their beds at five o'clock on the morning of Saturday 13 February 1692 and attempted to exterminate the four hundred clansmen who had been their hosts for two weeks.

The Massacre of Glen Coe was comparatively unsuccessful. Partly due to a blizzard which was raging at the time and partly because of Glenlyon's drunken incompetence and perhaps even partly because of the reluctance of the Highlanders in the Argyll regiment to betray their own traditions, only thirty-eight men including the old chief MacIain were killed. The rest of the clan fled into the hills, where many of the lightly clad women and children and the elderly perished in the snow. About half the clan escaped however.

There have been worse slaughterings among the clans in Highland history but Glen Coe remains in the memory because of the abuse of hospitality and because the killing was part of a political plot organised by John Dalrymple, The Master of Stair from London. When the Dutch King William succeeded the Stuart, James II and VII, after his abdication, the clan chiefs were required to swear an oath of loyalty to the new king or face 'the utmost extremity of the law'. The Highland chiefs had very precise and perhaps rather inflated notions of honour and most of them felt that they could not swear fealty to the new king without being relieved of their obligations to James, then in exile in France, to whom they had sworn support during the Jacobite rising of 1689 led by James Graham, Viscount Dundee. Threatened with extinction but with their concept of loyalty still intact, they appealed to the exiled king to release them from their oath to him so that they might swear loyalty to William. The date set for gaining the pardon by the swearing of loyalty to William was 1 January 1692.

The message from James at St Germain did not arrive in the Highlands until the last week of December 1691 and it said that the Jacobite chiefs might 'do what may be most for their own safety'. This did not leave much time for the chiefs to take the new oath before the Sheriffs of their shires, which in many cases required a long and arduous journey in the depths of winter. MacIain's oath-taking trip to Inveraray was delayed by a blizzard and a Campbell ambush at Barcaldine and complicated by the fact that the Sheriff-depute, Campbell of Ardkinglas, was across on the other side of Loch Fyne seeing in the New Year with his family. So MacIain took the oath six days late. Nevertheless Ardkinglas added his name to the list to be sent to Edinburgh for indemnity, appending a letter recommending its acceptance. In Edinburgh however (some say by a concourse of Campbell lawyers), MacIain's name was removed from the list before it was sent to the Privy Council.

Whether his name on the list would have saved the Glen Coe Macdonalds is a matter of doubt for it seems that, in London, Stair had already plotted their doom. 'For a just vengeance and a public example,' Stair had written to the Governor of Fort William, 'the thieving tribe of Glen Coe may be rooted out to a purpose.'

There is much more in the same vein in the voluminous papers concerning the Massacre and it seems certain that Campbell of Glenlyon was particularly selected to lead the Argyll regiment because he harboured a special enmity against the Glen Coe Macdonalds for a raid they had made on his property on the way back from the Battle of Killiecrankie. A good many of the Argylls were Campbells or septs of that clan and there was no love lost between the Campbells and the Macdonalds at any time. 'I desire you would begin with Glencoe and spare nothing which belongs to him,' Stair wrote to John Hill, the Governor of Fort William, 'but do not trouble the Government with prisoners.'

The echoes of that terrible order still seem to hang over the glen today. 'The Glen of Weeping,' Macaulay called it, though that was a fanciful, induced name — the author of the *Lays of Ancient Rome* was no Gaelic scholar. The Glen of Dogs is perhaps nearer the mark, for the legendary Fingal and his dogs hunted here and fought a great battle against the Vikings on the shores of Loch Leven. Above Loch Achtriochtan, in the middle of the glen, is the cave of Ossian, the bard of the Fingal epics, on the steep slopes of Aonach Dubh, part of the mountain ridge which shades the southern side of Glen Coe. Along the north rises the great 3,000-foot rock wall of Aonach Eagach. The Meeting of the Waters at the entry to the glen from the east, streams splashing over dark rocks to make the River Coe, is dominated by the two shepherd mountains, Buchaille Etive Beag and Buchaille Etive Mor, both over 3,000 feet. The stark splendour and the powerful, clenched rock faces of Glen Coe have a kind of ruthless beauty on a clear day and a true sense of doom which matches the glen's brutal history on a dark one.

There are testing rock climbs and ice faces to be negotiated in the Glen Coe ranges but there are also fine hill walks, eagles, ptarmigan, dotterel, deer and other animals such as the occasional wild cat to be seen. You can fish for trout on Loch Achtriochtan and on the River Coe.

Glen Coe was the National Trust for Scotland's first major holding in wild Highland country. With the help of the Scottish Mountaineering, Alpine and other climbing clubs, the Pilgrim Trust and the public, 12,800 acres of Glen Coe and the Forest of Dalness were bought between 1935 and 1937. The 1,390-acre farm of Achnacon was purchased from the Forestry Commission in 1972, with the help of a grant from the Countryside Commission for Scotland. Today Achnacon houses a laboratory for research into mountain safety, the Leishman Memorial Centre. There is a Visitor Centre at Clachaig.

So in Glen Coe the Trust's role is to preserve in its natural and unspoiled state

Canna.

the splendid wilderness country that this 14,200 acres represent. One of the major problems in what now is a very accessible area is litter and, at regular intervals, the Trust organises bands of volunteers to make sure that the majesty of the glen is not blighted by the modern detritus of urban civilisation.

It is also widely recognised that the Trust's work does much to encourage tourism. One way in which it is very directly involved in tourism is through the cruises which it has been running ever since the 1950s. Although these cruises do not confine their ports of call to places associated with Trust properties, many are always included in the voyage itineraries.

A typical National Trust for Scotland cruise on the Norwegian 9,500 tons *Black Prince*, used in winter by Fred Olsen Lines for service to the Canary Islands and Madeira, sailed from Leith in May 1984. Its first port was Kirkwall in the Orkneys where passengers had the opportunity to visit the great red twelfth-century cathedral of St Magnus, then on to the 4,500-year-old Neolithic tomb at Maes Howe and its contemporary village at Skara Brae, two of the oldest and best preserved prehistoric sites in Britain. Next day on to Ullapool on the west coast of Scotland and a chance to stroll through the Trust's amazing semi-tropical gardens at Inverewe, set in the same latitude as Labrador. Then the *Black Prince* sailed on to the once-banned island of Rhum, now a wildlife sanctuary and a living laboratory for the study of red deer; from there to the nearby islands of Mull and Iona, out to the deep Atlantic to the steep, seabird-thronged cliffs of St Kilda; north to the Faroes and Shetland and across the Norwegian Sea to the great sea-gash of the Nordfjord and a night in the colourful and charming port of Bergen, capital of West Norway and the birthplace of Scandinavia's greatest composer, Edvard Grieg; then home to Leith.

Every year the pattern of the voyage varies and in addition to the usual on-ship entertainments there are lectures on the places to be visited by experts in their subjects. These cruises are a special kind of experience and are so popular they sell out early. Full information about them can be had from Isabelle McLearie, Cruise Secretary at The National Trust for Scotland HS9/83C, 5 Charlotte Square, Edinburgh EH2 4DU. The Trust also makes arrangements for its members to join other cruises of architectural and historic interest in Europe and the Mediterranean.

An island which the *Black Prince* sailed past, distant on the western horizon beyond Rhum, is Canna, one of the Trust's most recent acquisitions. It is the outermost of the Inner Hebrides, south-west of the jagged rock outline of the Cuillins on Skye. It was transferred to the care of the National Trust of Scotland in 1981 by its owner, Dr John Lorne Campbell, the distinguished author and Gaelic scholar, who still lives there, working at Canna House in his unique library of Gaelic manuscripts and records, probably the most comprehensive collection of its kind in the world.

Mull: Pillared Basalt along the shore not far from MacCulloch's Tree. These formations are similar to the better known rocks of Staffa.

John Lorne Campbell has spent most of his life cherishing and preserving the Gaelic language and its records — and fighting for the often ignored rights of the people who speak that ancient language. When he lived on Barra in the 1930s he mounted a vigorous and disputatious campaign to close the Minch to trawlers and to protect the rights of the islanders to fish their own waters unchallenged. Later he led a rebellion on that island in which he incited the islanders not to pay any road tax on their cars until the county of Inverness set about making Barra's twelve miles of roads fit for the transit of motor vehicles. Dr Lorne Campbell is a formidable character, a meticulous and insatiable scholar, a fine writer and a man to be counted with a butterfly net or a billiard cue as well as a generous and welcoming host and a conversationalist of some pith and insight.

When he bought Canna in 1938, he brought with him to the island a young American musicologist, Margaret Fay, whom he had met in South Uist when she was conducting a study of Gaelic lore and music in South Uist. She became Mrs Campbell three years earlier. The comprehensive library of Celtic and Scots books and letters, the collection of manuscripts in and about Gaelic literature, life and customs, and the extensive recordings of song and story which form the Canna House library are a rich and priceless inheritance which is the work of both Dr Campbell and his wife. He is still working on it to ensure that when the ultimate control of this dedicated life of active scholarship, research and devotion finally passes from him, it will be as complete as possible.

There are just fifteen people on Canna and its adjacent, lower-lying island of Sanday, to which it is connected by a wooden bridge. There is no hotel, not even a boarding house, although the Trust lets out self-catering accommodation at *Tigh Ard* (the High House), built for the son and daughter of previous owners of the island, the Thoms. But it really has to be self-catering. You bring your own provisions with you because there is no shop on the island and everything has to come from Mallaig, twenty-six miles and two-and-a-half hours away by the Caledonian-MacBrayne Small Isles ferry, *Loch Mhor*, the island's only transport link with the mainland.

Not all the conservation projects of the National Trust for Scotland are as esoteric and scholarly as Dr Lorne Campbell's Gaelic library. On Canna, for example, as part of the Youth in Trust scheme, a pattern for involving young people in the work and aims of the Trust, youth groups come for a few days or longer periods to work on renovating the accommodation for visitors and helping farmer Iain Mackinnon to mend fences, restore some of the abandoned crofts and do other jobs needed by the island and its community.

Another function of the Trust is the letting of self-catering accommodation to holidaymakers in anything from a castle to a humble bothy. There are some thirty cottages and flats to let in Trust property, ranging in luxuriousness from The National Guest Flat in Culzean Castle in Ayrshire to a caravan in the grounds of

Craigievar Castle in Grampian.

The National Guest Flat at Culzean is in a rather special category. The tenure of this self-contained flat on the top floor of Ayrshire's most sumptuous castle was presented to General Dwight D Eisenhower in 1945 as a tribute to his service and his leadership of the Allied Forces as Supreme Commander at the end of the Second World War. General Eisenhower stayed in the flat several times (once when he was President of the United States) and often lent it to his friends for their use while they were visiting Scotland.

After his death, the National Trust for Scotland and Scottish Heritage USA collaborated to find a new use and function for this residence. Scottish Heritage USA is a non-profitmaking corporation founded in the United States in 1965 'to recognise and enhance the original bonds of ancestral and national character among the peoples of Scotland and North America'. It has greatly assisted the Trust's work since its foundation, particularly in relation to Culzean. It was decided that the flat could be used for Government hospitality and for important visitors concerned with the economic and social betterment of Scotland and the aims of the Trust.

It is a splendidly comfortable apartment at the head of the great oval staircase, one of Robert Adam's masterpieces of interior design. There are four double rooms, all with their own bathrooms, two twin-bedded rooms with a shared bathroom, a magnificent Round Drawing Room reflecting the lineaments and enhancing the view of Adam's great circular saloon immediately below, an elegant dining room with seating for sixteen people and, more intimately, a study which provides a personal link with Ike and his passion for golf (not an inappropriate enthusiasm in Ayrshire) in the paintings on the wall of Bobby Jones and the sixteenth hole at Augusta, where the US Masters is played.

The National Guest Flat is in a rather special category but anyone can apply to stay in other Trust properties which have accommodation. They include Gladstone's Land in Edinburgh, Hill of Tarvit near Cupar, Brodie Castle near Nairn, Craigievar Castle, Drum Castle, Haddo House, Leith Hall, Brodick Castle and cottages at Balmacara and Kintail. The Holidays Secretary, The National Trust for Scotland, 5 Charlotte Square, Edinburgh EH2 4DU will supply a booklet on the accommodation available on application.

Although the Trust is very far from being concerned only with stately homes, all the old buildings in its care have their problems. Many of these are tackled and resolved at workshops in and around Edinburgh. Over the door of Stenhouse Mansion in Gorgie Road, just four miles from the heart of Edinburgh, is a motto put here by Patrick Ellis, one of the early merchant-burgess lairds who had pretensions towards being a country gentleman. This gilded expression of gratitude, 'Blissit Be God for Al His Giftis', pious thought though it may be, is a somewhat ironical antithesis of the use to which the building has been put since

Gladstone's Land: Edinburgh.

1965. Within its venerable walls is a workshop — now run by the Historic Buildings and Monuments Directorate (Ancient Monuments) — where imperfect gifts acquired by the Trust are repaired and restored to something like their former glory. Stenhouse specialises in refurbishing and making new the decorative artefacts of other buildings, most of which belong to the same period as Stenhouse itself, the seventeenth century — painted ceilings, paintings and ornamental stonework.

Not all the work of the Trust comes from direct ownership of buildings and land. Some of it stems from Conservation Agreements operated by the Trust whereby an owner voluntarily enters into a pact with the Trust by which he still owns the buildings or the land but agrees not to alter it without the Trust's consent, thus preserving it for the future. In many cases this kind of agreement applies to substantial buildings, castles, historic monuments and sites and stately homes, but not always. The conditions under which Conservation Agreements are made vary considerably.

For example, The Old House in the charming village of New Abbey in Kirkcudbrightshire is a property of just one acre but it helps to preserve the character of the village, which is dominated by the magnificent red sandstone ruin of Sweetheart Abbey, built by Devorgilla, the wife of John Balliol, founder of Balliol College in Oxford, and the mother of the 'Toom Tabard', the other John Balliol, the puppet king appointed to rule Scotland by Edward I of England. In the churchyard of Sweetheart Abbey too is the burial place of William Paterson, one of the founders of the Bank of England and the chief motivator of Scotland's last and most disastrous attempt at colonisation, the Darien Scheme of 1698.

There had been attempts before in Nova Scotia, New England and Carolina where Scots merchants had tried to break the trade monopoly on the colonies established by the English. Although the two countries were united under one king (the first, ironically, the son of the murdered Mary, Queen of Scots, James I of England and VI of Scotland) there were still separate parliaments for England and Scotland and the Scots and the English regarded each other as foreigners. When in 1695 William Paterson set up the Company of Scotland trading to Africa and the Indies, proposed as a joint Scots and English company in London, the English trading companies, particularly the East India Company, vehemently opposed the idea, impeaching the founders for treachery before the House of Commons!

The Scots Parliament and the people of Scotland were furious. The report of the Commission of Enquiry into the Massacre of Glen Coe was still being awaited in Edinburgh and the Scots were in no mood to brook further English tyranny. 'Money will beget money,' Paterson said, 'trade will increase trade.' The idea of trading to Africa was abandoned and a site for the New Caledonia was chosen in the Isthmus of Panama on the coast of Darien — a place to which none of its advocates as a suitable site for a colony had ever been. Their information came largely from the journals of a young buccaneer-surgeon named Lionel Wafer as well as through tales of its conquest almost two hundred years before by the Spanish *conquistador*, Vasco Nunez de Balboa, who discovered the Pacific Ocean for the west. (Keat's 'Stout Cortez . . . silent upon a peak in Darien' is an historical inaccuracy, unworthy of a man who had just been looking into Chapman's *Homer*! Cortez was the conqueror of Mexico and he did not arrive in mainland America until three years after Balboa had sighted the Pacific in 1513.)

Paterson and his fellow directors ignored Wafer's description of Darien as 'one of the wettest places in the world', ignored the fact that on the first expedition to the isthmus in 1509, the Spaniards had suffered the severest losses of their imperial venture to that date from hunger, fever and the poisoned arrows of the native Indians. They also seem to have completely discounted the fact that Spain might have any entitlement to the place and that the Spanish claim to Darien had been recognised by William III and the English Parliament.

Despite all these factors, national sentiment and fury against the English ensured that the Darien expedition was heavily subscribed. More than £400,000 — an immense sum in the 1690s, said to be half the available capital of the Scots nation — came in from individuals, corporations, burghs and associations; ships were bought or chartered from the continent and a very odd assortment of goods were assembled in warehouses. It was believed that these could be traded for the gold and silver, spices and silks which were expected to be found in Darien.

The expedition sailed from Leith in July 1698 and arrived off the coast of Darien in November, many of the would-be colonists of the New Caledonia already dead or ill with fever and other diseases. The Spaniards attempted to retake the 'colony' three times and only succeeded on the fourth attempt. No assistance was offered to 'New Caledonia' by the English colonies in America and the Caribbean and in April 1700, the 'colony' was abandoned with the terrible loss of two thousand lives and all the money and goods invested in its creation. Only three hundred of the colonists, soldiers and seamen who had sailed to Darien with such high hopes returned to Scotland.

Scotland was angry, impoverished and despairing and, despite the incompetence shown in the planning and organising and equipping of the expeditions, despite the petty squabbling among the colonial leaders, the blind ignorance of the site chosen and the terrible inexperience which caused so many minor disasters to escalate into calamity, the nation blamed it on the English. It was in this unhappy climate of opinion that negotiations were entered into for the absorption of the Scottish Parliament into the Parliament at Westminster.

Although it is sometimes claimed that Scotland lost much and was bribed,

Turret House: Kelso.

bamboozled and betrayed into the Union of Parliaments in 1707, not all was taken nor abandoned. As Tennyson says as Ulysses:

Tho' much is taken, much abides; and tho'
We are not now that strength which in old days
Moved earth and heaven; that which we are, we are;
One equal temper of heroic hearts
Made weak by time and fate, but strong in will
To strive, to seek, to find and not to yield.

Amid all the conniving, bluster, riot and double-dealing of 1707, there were several things that were not yielded. The Scottish Parliament vanished to Westminster to form a Parliament of Great Britain in which Scotland's representation was forty-five members against five hundred and thirteen Englishmen, with sixteen Scottish peers elected to sit in the House of Lords; but the law, Scottish courts and legal code and the Kirk remained, the royal burghs kept their privileges and a morsel of Scottish identity was statutorily maintained. Otherwise, today there would not exist particular Scottish institutions like the National Trust for Scotland.

3

THE SOUTH-WEST

THE SOLWAY FIRTH is the south-western edge of Scotland, where the gentle shore resorts of Kirkcudbrightshire and the hills of Galloway look across to England. The broad estuary of the Solway is never lively. Its towns and villages and seascapes are favourites with painters but no great highways pass along its coast. The road to Edinburgh goes up the east coast; the motorways to Glasgow and the west lie fifteen miles to the other side of Dumfries. Only the discriminating and the knowledgeable turn off the main road at Gretna and head west. Attempts to turn the Solway coast into the Scottish Riviera have always been a bit half-hearted.

But the south-west is the land of the warrior king, Robert the Bruce, who liberated Scotland from English domination in the fourteenth century, and the home country of the the poet, Robert Burns, who gave Scotland its literary identity at the end of the 1700s and whose poems are known and whose songs are sung all over the world. There is moorland and mountain in Galloway, rich farmland in Ayrshire. One of the finest panoramas in Britain from its ocean coast stretches from the hammerhead peninsula of the Rhinns of Galloway to Farland Head, overlooking the mountainous outline of Arran, the granite bulk of Ailsa Craig and the long finger of the Mull of Kintyre guarding it against the Atlantic.

There is history and wild country, long gentle seascapes over the Firth, stern cliffs against the Atlantic breakers and one of the finest houses in Scotland at the southern end of Ayrshire's golf-course-dappled shoreline. And, although comparatively few tourists come to the south-west, at least the Galloway shore, in late autumn has other visitors. Along the great shallow estuary of the Solway Firth which divides Scotland from England on the west coast, the wildfowl wheel and settle; rest and feed on their long journeys from the Arctic and Siberia to their winter quarters in Scotland and Europe.

At Threave, below the ancient islanded castle, a Douglas stronghold dating from the fourteenth century on the River Dee in Kirkcudbrightshire, the National Trust for Scotland has a wildfowl refuge. From November to March, thousands of birds — greylag geese, the ancestors of the domestic goose, whitefronts and pinkfeet, barnacle, Brents and Canadas, tufted ducks, mallard, teal, pintails and shovellers goldeneyes and goosanders with grebes and cormorants and herons — throng these sheltered waters. There are hides from which to watch them but the birds are not lured nor fed neither are they collected. This is a refuge in the true sense.

When the Threave estate was given to the Trust in 1948 by Major A F Gordon, establishing the area as a wildfowl refuge was a prime purpose of its gift. But Threave House and its gardens, a beautiful place to wander about among the ponds and plants, flower beds and blossoming trees, have been put to good use. For the gardens at Threave are not just for looking at but for learning as well. Here, quartered in Threave House, youngsters, not just from Britain but from all over the world, learn the art and craft of being gardeners under the expert tuition of the Principal, Bill Hean.

The Threave School of Gardening was opened in 1960 and sixteen young people from seventeen to twenty years old take its two-year course designed to give them a comprehensive basic training in both practical and theoretical aspects of horticulture. Since 1960 the gardens themselves — originally just one acre of walled garden — have evolved from the practical instruction of students. Today Threave incorporates a rose garden, a woodland garden, a walled garden with patio, a rock garden, nursery, vegetable gardens, a pond with herbaceous beds, an arboretum and heather garden and a sunken garden.

Just a few miles to the north-west of where the rivers Sark and Esk flow into the broad estuary which becomes the Solway Firth is the birthplace of a man who should have loved gardens. 'Manufacture is intelligible but trivial. Creation is great and cannot be understood,' he wrote in one of the celebrated essays which made him an intellectual giant of the nineteenth century.

Thomas Carlyle was born in the now quiet village of Ecclefechan, just a few miles north of the border with England, in 1795 in the Arched House, a good example of a late eighteenth-century craftsman's village home, built with a kind of rustic elegance by his stonemason father and uncle in two wings above a pend. From the village he walked the 82 miles to Edinburgh University at the age of thirteen in order to enlarge his formidable array of learning.

Formidable is the apt word for Carlyle, historian, essayist, social reformer and prophet who became one of the major influences on nineteenth-century British thought with his clarion call for moral fidelity, hard work, social reform and the reconstruction of living patterns, the revival of religion and sincerity in dealings between human beings.

Threave Castle.

Carlyle's belief in the virtues of authority did not endear him to everyone in a restless and revolutionary age but he had an impressive clarity of vision into the essence of moral and social problems. In *Past and Present* and *The French Revolution*, in pages growling with the menace of the hungry poor, he places the responsibility for mass hardship firmly where it belongs — on the ruling classes. Although some of his contemporaries felt that his concept of social morality and its patterns was too arid (One of them said, 'Carlyle has led us out into the desert — and he has left us there.'), his reiteration of the basic virtues of piety, hard work and moral integrity had a profound effect not only in Britain but in Europe and he is one of the great figures of his age.

The Arched House contains a collection of manuscripts, relics and mementoes of a half-remembered great man, among them a very handsome rosewood writing case given to Carlyle by Mrs Lytton Strachey, several portraits and Jane Welsh's mother's best china. His mother was proud of him and, touchingly, learned to write in middle age so that she could personally decipher the letters from her famous son sent her from London.

Carlyle's stern philosophy and learned discourses on moral and historic problems may be out of fashion nowadays but the simple qualities he admired seem to linger on in this building. The books exemplify his pride in learning, the plain but not inelegant furniture his stoic tastes. His barbed humour is more difficult to illustrate — I have always thought that the Ministry of Transport in urban areas might well take as their text the Carlylean aphorism: 'the public highways ought not to be occupied by people demonstrating that motion is impossible' — but it is there along with the thunderous denunciations and the fiery imaginative leaps in his writings.

He lived to be eighty-six and is buried with his parents in Hoddom Churchyard just up the road. He refused the offer of Westminster Abbey before

Carlyle's Birthplace.

Carlyle's Birthplace: a room.

he died and there is a famous Victorian print of his funeral in the house. He wished to be remembered as a prophet, not a writer, but his vision of a benignly authoritarian society remains unfulfilled and his books today are largely unread except by scholars. Yet the novelist, George Eliot (Mary Ann Evans, no great admirer of authoritarianism) said of him: 'There is hardly a superior or active mind of this generation that has not been modified by Carlyle's writing, there has hardly been an English book written for the last ten or twelve years that would not have been different if Carlyle had not lived.'

Although he lived for a long period in Chelsea in London and travelled abroad, the countryside in which he was born was always dear to him and he always came back, perhaps to refresh his experience of one of his most pithy epigrams from *The Hero as a Man of Letters*: 'Adversity is sometimes hard upon a man; but for one man who can stand prosperity, there are a hundred that will stand adversity.'

The most spectacular of the Trust's countryside properties in the south-west has links with a Carlyle hero, Sir Walter Scott, of whom he said, 'No sounder piece of British manhood was put together in that eighteenth century of Time.' Riding in the trackless hinterland above the waterfall of The Grey Mare's Tail on the road between Moffat and Selkirk, Scott 'went down, horse and man, into a bog-hole and was hard-put to get extricated'.

This wilderness countryside, no less empty today than it was when it served as a refuge for fleeing Covenanters in the seventeenth century, is a wedge of 2,383 acres which provides access to White Coomb, at 2,696 feet one of the highest peaks in the Southern Uplands. The wildflowers around the waterfall are particularly colourful and the fall itself with its 200-foot white plume of water against the grey and green of the hillside is dramatic. This is rough country where you have to move with care, populated only by the perennial sheep and wild goats. 'The sheep,' says the National Trust for Scotland Guide, 'are not aggressive'.

Aggression, on the other hand, was Robert the Bruce's forte. Going westward over Galloway, another bit of history preserved by the Trust is Bruce's Stone in a forest clearing beside Clatteringshaws Loch, where the Scottish king rested after the Battle of Moss Raploch in 1307, one of his first victories in his campaign to free Scotland from the English.

Bruce came across the sea from Ulster to begin his war of liberation but in his native Carrick he never found anything as splendid as Culzean Castle, Robert Adam's masterpiece, built at the end of the eighteenth century for the 10th Earl of Cassilis. It perches majestically on the rim of the Carrick cliffs looking out across the broadening Firth of Clyde towards Ailsa Craig, Arran, the Mull of Kintyre and the Atlantic. Here, setting and style combine in a unique way.

The castle is sumptuously decorated and elegantly designed within and without. The Armoury at the entrance bristles with weapons in elaborate display forms, most of which were issued to the West Lowland Fencibles, a regiment raised by the 12th Earl of Cassilis in the early years of the nineteenth century to combat the threat of invasion by Napoleon Bonaparte. The old Eating Room with vine-leaves and grape clusters in the plaster friezes is now a sitting room but still has the original Adam mirrors and some fine eighteenth-century furniture. The Dining Room next door has some of the furniture originally designed for the Eating Room, a Derby dessert service, Chinese porcelain and a selection of family portraits as well as two busts reflecting the nineteenth-century preoccupation of the Kennedy family with Napoleon — white marble heads of the French emperor and his second wife, Marie Louise of Austria.

The great oval staircase is one of Adam's finest achievements, the wide spiral of elaborately balustraded and pillared stairs rising to the glass cupola, the cunning use of the thicker, more richly decorated Corinthian columns, bristling with acanthus leaves on the first floor, and the slimmer, whorl-topped Ionic columns on the second, exaggerating the dramatic effect.

There are fine pictures everywhere. The Picture Room on the first floor has the famous paintings of Culzean itself by Alexander Nasmyth, 'the father of

Side Chair, c. 1745, Irish, Mahogany with needlework cover from Culzean Castle.

Scottish landscape' and the portraitist of Robert Burns. There is a portrait of David Kennedy, 10th Earl of Cassilis, who commissioned Robert Adam to rebuild Culzean, by the fashionable Italian painter, Pompeo Batoni, some fine Dutch landscapes and seascapes and an impressive portrait of Napoleon by Lefevre in the Best Bedroom on the first floor.

Equally splendid is the furniture. Chairs, beds and tables designed by great English craftsmen like Hepplewhite, Sheraton and Chippendale, French pieces from the periods of Louis XV and XVI, mirrors, candle sconces, furniture, carpets and ornaments designed by Adam himself. The magnificently decorated ceilings of intricate painted plasterwork in the principal rooms are echoed by matching Adam-designed carpets.

The Saloon on the first floor is one of the most superbly conceived rooms even Robert Adam ever designed. The fastidious symmetry of eighteenth-century elegance in this circular room with its finely moulded ceiling, beautiful hangings, fine pictures and giltwood chairs and the carpet with the Cassilis swans woven into the border of the design which Adam created especially for this room is contrasted with the view from the tall windows, of the sea breaking on the rocks 150 feet below, the peaks of Arran, the low peninsula of Kintyre and the granite hump of Ailsa Craig, in a perfect blend of designed emotional response.

In fact the carpet is new, specially woven by Craigie Carpets in Irvine and generously donated by the Hoover Foundation, and the ceiling has been restored and repainted in its pristine colours. But the designs are those which Robert Adam created for this particular room. The normal process of renewal has been followed faithfully.

Throughout the castle there are fascinating touches of domesticity, like the slipper bath with its attendant hot and cold water cans; the delightful boat-shaped cradle and the Kennedy obsession with Napoleon, as emphasised again by the best bedroom portrait.

But Napoleon is not the only great commander to have links with Culzean. The Kennedy family who are the Earls of Cassilis and have ruled this coast for centuries are related to Robert the Bruce, who was himself a Carrick man. But the main martial connection is more modern. In 1945, when Culzean was offered to the National Trust for Scotland, there came with the offer the proposal that General Eisenhower, Supreme Commander of the victorious Allied Forces in Europe should be given the life tenure of the top floor of the castle. Eisenhower accepted and stayed there several times, once when he was President of the United States. On the first floor, next to the magnificent saloon in the drum tower, there is an Eisenhower Room which houses an exhibition celebrating his life and achievements.

The Eisenhower flat, the National Trust Flat for Scotland, is today let out to important guests — a splendidly comfortable apartment at the head of the

Souter Johnnie's Cottage, Kirkoswald, Ayrshire.

great oval staircase. The magnificent Round Drawing Room reflects the lineaments and has an even more magnificent view over the sea and islands than Adam's great circular saloon immediately below.

As part of his plan for Culzean, just along the cliff from the castle, Robert Adam designed a graceful, Italianate home farm which has now become the centre of Culzean's other multifarious activities. Curiously enough, these devolved from disaster.

When the 5th Marquess of Ailsa (the Earls of Cassilis became marquesses in 1830) offered Culzean to the National Trust for Scotland in 1945, it was without an endowment. In its commendable enthusiasm to preserve such a property, the Trust accepted. But, as the years passed, despite brave efforts to raise money, it became clear that Culzean, regarded by many as the greatest treasure in the Trust's care, was so far from making ends meet that it threatened to become a financial burden of ruinous extent. It was saved in 1969 by becoming Scotland's first Country Park.

The home farm has become a visitor centre with a restaurant, exhibition space, audio-visual guide to Culzean, shop and a centre for youth activities. The three miles of fascinating coastline above which the castle towers on its cliff, offer a chance to explore the shore and learn about the marine life of the Firth of Clyde. There are miles of woodland walks, play areas and an adventure playground, picnic areas, a deer park and an aviary, and a programme of walks guided by rangers. As Michael Tebbutt, the Trust's amiable and enthusiastic administrator at Culzean says, 'It is not just one of the finest houses in Britain but a day out for all the family'.

Today Culzean is the most active of all the Trust's properties with an enormous range of things to do and around 300,000 visitors a year. In addition to all the amenities already mentioned, it hosts events ranging from private dinner parties to Children's Weeks, stunning fireworks displays and a country fair. It is genial public hospitality exemplified.

Just up the road in the village of Kirkoswald is a link with over-genial hospitality gone wrong — Souter Johnnie's Cottage. John Davidson was the village cobbler — the souter — and he moved into the thatched cottage which is now one of the National Trust's properties, in 1785. Five years after he acquired the cottage, the Kirkoswald cobbler had immortality thrust upon him when Robert Burns, in a single day at Ellisland in Dumfriesshire, wrote his great narrative poem, *Tam O'Shanter*, that rumbustious, vivid and humorous account of a Carrick farmer's encounter with the Devil. At the drinking session which precedes Tam's ride to the haunted kirk of Alloway, there was:

> *At his elbow, Souter Johnnie,*
> *His ancient trusty, drouthy cronie:*
> *Tam lo'ed him like a very brither*
> *They had been fou for weeks thegither.*

Burns had stayed at Kirkoswald, where his mother was born, when he was sixteen to study mathematics and land-surveying with Hugh Rodger, the local dominie. By his own account Burns made 'pretty good progress' in his mensuration studies, 'but I made greater progress in the knowledge of mankind'. At the end of the eighteenth century, Kirkoswald was one of the centres of the smuggling trade, which brought in illicit goods from the continent and the Isle of Man, and boatloads of whisky from the Highlands. The young Burns mixed with the smugglers and saw, as he later wrote, 'scenes of swaggering riot and roaring dissipation'.

Persistent tradition has it that John Davidson is the original of Souter Johnnie, just as Douglas Graham, tenant of Shanter farm nearby, a celebrated roysterer even in this smuggling country, was the model for Tam himself.

The cottage contains a typical collection of local furniture and the tools and

The Bachelors' Club, Tarbolton, Ayrshire.

implements of a village cobbler, including a special chair, almost certainly used by the Souter himself. Here too is the Souter's family Bible, double box beds and a fine set of Glasgow blue and white china. Out in the garden at the back another building of the time has been reconstructed as a heather-thatched alehouse to provide a home for the life-size stone figures of the Souter, Tam and the innkeeper and his wife, swapping stories over the ale and listening to the fiddle. These vivid figures were made in 1802 by James Thom, a self-taught sculptor from another village with which Burns was very familiar, Tarbolton, seventeen miles to the north.

Burns' Masonic badge is in Souter Johnnie's cottage and the place where the poet became a mason, the Bachelors' Club in Tarbolton, is also a property of the National Trust for Scotland. Here Burns first went to dancing classes — 'to improve my manners,' he said — but other motives, not unconnected with the bright-eyed lassies to whose wiles he was so susceptible, have been suspected. Here too in 1780, the year before he was initiated into the rites of Freemasonry, with his brother Gilbert and five other young men, he formed the Bachelors' Club, a debating society for any 'cheeful, honest-hearted lad, who, if he has a friend that is true, and a mistress that is kind, and as much wealth as genteely make both ends meet — is just as happy as this world can make him'. The first subject of debate was whether to marry for looks or money. There is not much doubt about which side the author of *My love is like a red, red rose* was on.

Downstairs in this seventeenth-century two-storey building there is an authentic period kitchen and upstairs the room where the Bachelors' Club and Tarbolton Freemasons used to meet has been restored to its former use with an old oak refectory table, country-made chairs and suitable period items. Here, every January, is held the only Burns Supper in the world in a setting which the poet himself would recognise, attended by distinguished guests from all over the world, Americans, Russians and expatriate Scots among them.

There are more books about Robert Burns than anyone else except Jesus Christ and William Shakespeare — literally thousands of them — and his poems have been translated into at least twenty languages. From this little room where he met with his friends when he was twenty-one, his international reputation sprang, although his own vision of internationalism still lacks fulfilment:

> *Then let us pray that come it may*
> *As come it will for a' that*
> *That sense and worth o'er a' the earth*
> *May bear the gree for a' that.*
> *For a' that and a' that*
> *It's coming yet for a' that*
> *That man to man, the warld o'er*
> *Shall brothers be for a' that.*

4

GLASGOW AND THE WEST

THE POPULAR conception of Glasgow and the West, the industrial heartland of Scotland, does not evoke many images of scenic splendour. But along the banks of the River Clyde, once the greatest shipbuilding river in the world and the birthplace of battleships and great Transatlantic liners, there is everything Scotland has to show of the different ways in which people live and have lived. From tenements to castles, gardens to mountains, salmon rivers to sea lochs, the accent is on variety.

Helensburgh, on the Firth of Clyde, overlooks the point at which the great river turns south to run into the Atlantic. It is the birthplace of John Logie Baird, whose electronic experiments gave the world its first practical demonstrations of television. It was also a fashionable place for rich Glasgow businessmen to live within easy commuting distance of the city and it has many substantial family homes on the hillside above the river.

The finest of them is The Hill House, Glasgow architect Charles Rennie Mackintosh's greatest achievement in domestic architecture — a house he built which still contains the furniture he designed for it. This pale grey, harled, pewter-slated house with its pepper-pot turret at one end, its curves and angles, cliff-like walls and soaring, tapering chimneys at the other is a splendid example of Mackintosh's style, a kind of contemporary modification of Scottish vernacular tradition and a highly decorative sensibility.

The more familiar aspects of Mackintosh's idiosyncratic style first appear in the gates leading to the house, in the trellised cross forms of the wrought-iron decoration with their suggestion of medieval sconces. The house was commissioned by the publisher, Walter Blackie, in 1902 and passed out of private ownership in 1972. It came to the National Trust for Scotland from the trust established by the Royal Incorporation of Architects in Scotland, and it was

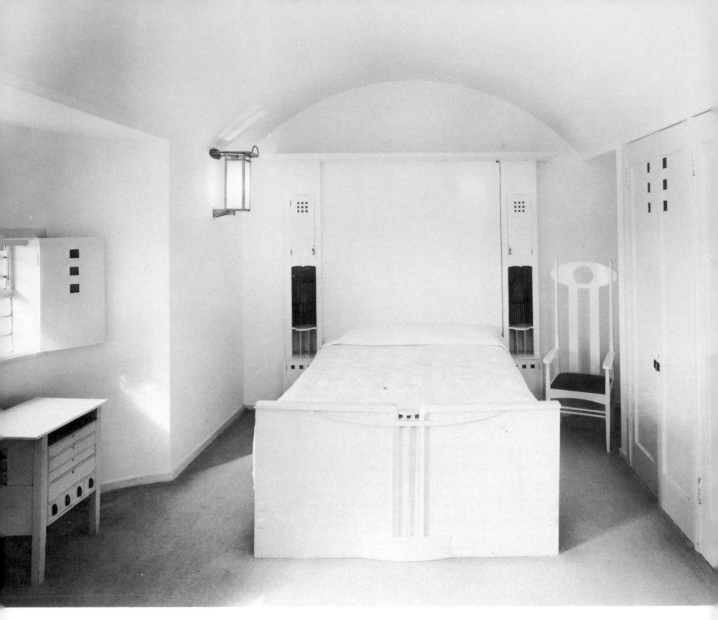

The Hill House: Bedroom.

acquired just in time, for the house had fallen into a sad state of deterioration and needed extensive work done on it. With the help of the National Heritage Memorial Fund, the National Trust of Scotland took over The Hill House and began restoring it to its former glory.

Inside the entrance hall the staircase soars upwards in dark, narrowing shafts of wood. The offset geometric patterns are repeated everywhere. On doors, cupboards, wardrobes, carpets and curtains, even in a simple black and white clock face in the hall, decorative and stylish but a little hard to read! Not all is geometric however. At the top of many of the tapering straight lines there is a sudden blossoming of shape and colour, often a stylised flower. Mackintosh was fascinated by the decorative application of formalised plant life.

But it was not all decoration. Charles Rennie Mackintosh made a careful study of how the Blackies lived and his elegant and striking designs had purpose as well as line and colour. In the library, for example, now used as the reception area for the house, there is even a custom-built cupboard for Blackie's pipes which he used to smoke as he read manuscripts for his publishing firm. In the bathroom the bath and shower fittings were specially designed by Mackintosh. The all-round shower which sprays water not just from the top but from the semi-circular pipes at the side is believed to be the first shower of its type ever installed in a Scottish house. The main bedroom is a singularly beautiful and striking room, almost totally white with the elegant wardrobes just touched with pink rose heads, small cupboards beside the bed for books and the tall, severe ladderback chairs serving almost as punctuation marks for the design.

The Hill House: Drawing Room.

In spite of its innovative design features, it was a house to be lived in and it is as such that it is fondly remembered by Blackie's daughters, Agnes and her sister, Mrs Hedderwick, who spent their childhood there. 'My recollection,' said Agnes Blackie, 'is of a lovely feeling of space and light as a little girl and the feeling that you could run from end to end and that sort of thing. Just a general feeling of room. I never thought it peculiar at all,' she added. 'Just my home. So little so that when, at some later stage, I was in Glasgow and somebody took me to tea in Miss Cranston's Room de Luxe, I just thought — this is really like home!'

Mrs Hedderwick was nostalgic about the house. 'I feel rather sad that it is not a lived in house any more, because it was such a very nice house to live in — and it wasn't, I don't think, a frightfully difficult house to run.'

Agnes Blackie was more definite. 'I'd rather it wasn't lived in than lived in by people I didn't like,' she said with some asperity. 'I always remember my father saying rather wistfully that perhaps the National Trust will take it over. So, though I have reservations, thinking of the places that are now just more or less museums, the rooms that are museum pieces, I do always remember my father saying that, which makes it seem as if it has come full circle in a way.'

The Tenement House at 145 Buccleuch Street in Garnethill above Sauchiehall Street in Glasgow is a very different kind of home from the sculptured elegance of Mackintosh's The Hill House in Helensburgh. The first-floor flat in this red

The Tenement House: Parlour.

The Tenement House: Parlour.

sandstone tenement building preserves, as if in amber, a segment of Glasgow life spreading back for almost a hundred years to 1892. It was saved by the good eye and good sense of a girl who went there with her uncle who had been left a few Victorian dining-room chairs in the owners's will.

Agnes Toward lived almost all her life in this flat. When she died in 1975 she left these six dining-room chairs to her church elder, Dr Sam Davidson, one of her few visitors. Dr Davidson took his niece, a young actress, Anna Davidson, along with him to collect them. Anna was so fascinated by the flat and its myriad contents, recognising that it represented a unique example of Glasgow life, that she bought it complete with contents.

Miss Toward had lived with her mother at 145 Buccleuch Street since she had been a teenager and after her mother's death she lived there alone. There are two rooms with a kitchen and a bathroom. Miss Toward made absolutely no attempt to modernise her home, the original furniture and fittings are still there —thanks to Anna Davidson. The closed kitchen range, sink and coal box are as they were when the flat was built. The box beds are original. Also, Miss Toward was a kind of human magpie who never threw anything away. There are calendars, postcards, tram, theatre and rail tickets, cuttings from newspapers and recipes which give the flavour of life in Glasgow over almost a century.

Anna lived there happily for six years, cleaning up the flat but preserving

The Tenement House: Bedroom.

everything that Agnes Toward had left behind. When, because of her acting commitments, she had to move, she persuaded the National Trust for Scotland to buy it for the marvellous impression it gave of life in Glasgow over the last eighty years.

You can get only twelve people at a time into this tenement flat but it represents a very different aspect of Scottish life to that depicted by most Trust properties.

The Tenement House is now visited by many schoolchildren so that they can see how their grannies lived — but there is more room in a garden and, on the south side of Glasgow, in Greenbank Garden, the educational emphasis is horticultural rather than sociological.

Jim May, the Trust's resident gardening instructor in this two and a half acres of walled garden around an elegant Georgian house, gives weekly gardening lessons and hints in courses of instruction specially aimed at owners of small gardens. There is also special instruction in gardening crafts tailored to the needs and abilities of disabled gardeners.

A few miles to the south-west of Glasgow a different kind of craft is the focal point in Kilbarchan, a village just outside Johnstone. The Weaver's Cottage is one of the original houses of the village of Kilbarchan and was built at the beginning of the eighteenth century. From the end of the seventeenth century, Kilbarchan

Greenbank: Glasgow.

was a weaving community making cambrics, muslins and lawns, gingham and repp as well as linens and woollen fabrics. The handlooms on the ground floor, complete with reeds and shuttles, spinning and pirn wheels, are still in use and on show are examples of the tools of the trade and of Kilbarchan weaving — shoulder shawls, tartans, shirt material, Paisley shawls in silk. Some of the shawls are shown on for the box beds — of which there are a large number in the house. In the nineteenth century Kilbarchan was making ponchos for the United States, Egypt and South America, an exotic trade it would seem for a Renfrewshire village.

This memorial museum to the weavers of Kilbarchan was created by the local community, who contributed many of the items it contained when the Trust restored the cottage to its original character in 1957. Built in 1723, it is a fine example of the cruck structure system, where the weight of the roof is carried not by walls but by a wooden framework of tree-trunk tresses, clearly seen on the top floor — the forerunner of the modern steel-framed building. That Kilbarchan was a pretty independent community which fed as well as clothed itself, can be seen from the cheese presses, an oatcake toaster, a peat oven and a beebole in the wall to take three skeps of bees.

Kilbarchan is just off the road to Ardrossan, the port of embarkation for the island of Arran, one of the West of Scotland's favourite holiday resort. The folk of the west — or at least those of them who go to Arran — do not like their holiday places to have esplanades, illuminations, imitation Eiffel Towers, red-nosed comedians nor candy floss stalls and the pleasures of Arran are the simple ones of sea and shoreline, mountain and moorland, with a few golf courses, tennis courts and some sea and river fishing thrown in for extra measure.

Arran is a dramatic and highly scenic island with high mountains, fine beaches, small white-washed cottages and stone villages clustered along its coastline which faces west to Argyll and the Atlantic on one side and east to the Ayrshire coast and the Firth of Clyde on the other.

The National Trust for Scotland has two related properties on Arran, the splendidly furnished Brodick Castle with a lovely garden between its walls and the sea and, at its back, a mountain, Goatfell. The name has nothing to do either with goats or falling but in Gaelic means 'The Mountain of the Winds'. At 2,866 feet it is the highest peak on the island and in May there is a race up this tough and rugged mountain — about as strenuous a way to spend an island Saturday as can be imagined. Most people prefer to take it more quietly and there are organised walks on Goatfell's 7,300 acres, starting from the castle at the foot. A ranger guide accompanies the party and explains the special features of the mountain.

There is a relatively easy path to the top of Goatfell and the Trust's representative reckons that some 10,000 people climb it every year, many of whom have never climbed a mountain before. But there are tougher ways up

Goatfell than by the path; for more solitary hillwalkers there is good rock- — from the Ayrshire coast and the huge sweep of the Firth of Clyde and the great peaks beyond to the mountains of Argyll and the long tongue of Kintyre reaching south towards the coast of Ulster.

In July, 1889, Goatfell acquired a more sinister reputation when it was the scene of what became known as the Arran murder. A Glasgow pattern-maker, John Watson Laurie, on holiday in Arran with Edwin Robert Rose, an English friend of just a few days acquaintanceship, battered Rose to death while climbing the mountain and threw his body into *Coire man Fuaran* — the Gully of Fire, a corrie on the north side of the twin Goatfell peaks. At least, that is the common assumption. The case even eclipsed the seventh murder of Jack the Ripper in London in public interest and when Laurie was arrested after a bizarre few weeks on the run during which he wrote to the newspapers protesting his innocence, thousands of people besieged the High Court in Edinburgh to attend his trial. Amazingly, he was reprieved after being sentenced to death. He spent forty-one years in prison, dying in 1930 and taking with him to his grave the terrible secret of what really happened on that July day on the Mountain of the Winds.

In contrast to the savage and sordid story of the Arran murder and its dramatic primitive setting, Brodick Castle at the foot of the mountain could hardly be more civilised. Rebuilt in the nineteenth century by Scots architect, Gillespie Graham, it continued the pattern in red sandstone of the existing buildings — mostly sixteenth-century with a few thirteenth century stones, and a wing added by Oliver Cromwell to serve as a battery and garrison accommodation during the invasion of Scotland in 1651. The eastern tower is the oldest part and, to a degree, it set the pattern for the rest, rather severe and baronial on the outside.

Inside, however, all is very different. Although there are certainly reminders of the great outdoors in the eighty-seven stags' heads in the entrance hall, all but one (which came from Hungary) red deer shot on the island, the interior emphasis is on rich and unusual furnishings, porcelain, paintings, silver and *objets d'art* —and more than a hint of recklessness.

The Hamiltons owned Brodick Castle and most of Arran from 1503 until it was handed over to the National Trust for Scotland at the wish of Mary Louise, Duchess of Montrose (who had been born a Hamilton) after her death in 1957. Down the centuries they had always been gamblers — for thrones, power, wealth and, in the nineteenth century, on horses, cards, prize-fighters, bear-baiting and the like. In the early days this compulsion sometimes cost them their heads — in the nineteenth century merely their fortunes. Luckily, at that time, these were considerable. Being just a heartbeat from the throne of Scotland by their descent from James II was sometimes too big a temptation in the sixteenth century but it did give them an international cachet and last century they added to the family coffers and status by marrying well.

The 11th Duke married Princess Marie of Baden, whose mother had been the Empress Josephine's niece and the adopted daughter of Napoleon. Lady Mary, the 12th Duke's sister, married Prince Albert of Monaco and later a Hungarian prince, Count Tassilo Festetics de Tolna, who shot the largest stag on display in the entrance hall.

Arguably, however, the best of the Hamilton matches was made by the 10th Duke who married Susan Euphemia Beckford, daughter and heiress to William Beckford of Fonthill, himself heir to a great merchant fortune, eccentric to the point of perversion, author of a curious oriental Faustian novel, *Caliph Vathek*, connoisseur and manic collector.

Beckford inherited a vast fortune made in the West Indies. A strange, sensitive, artistic and precocious child, he had composition lessons from Mozart when he was five — Wolfgang Amadeus being then nine — and there is something at once touching and slightly mad in the vision of these two children in the grave relationship of pupil and master, that is typical of the whole complex Beckford saga. His wide-ranging education developed considerable artistic taste and discrimination, often in largely unexplored fields, and he collected everything with an opulent magpie enthusiasm.

Although his collection has been diminished from time to time as the Beckford wealth sallied forth again and again to save the Hamiltons from their gambling debts, Brodick still houses the finest Beckford collection in the world —paintings, pottery, furniture, silver and silver-mounted objects in half a hundred styles and traditions which he collected on his travels round the world.

But the Beckford collection by no means exhausts the riches of Brodick Castle — although the sporting prints of horse-races and prize-fights, paintings like Herrings, *Dirtiest Derby* and the many sporting trophies won by the Hamilton

Pair of Thistle Mugs, c. 1692 from Brodick Castle, Isle of Arran.

Provan Hall: Glasgow.

racehorses (seven St Leger winners in twenty-eight years as well as the 1867 Grand National) provide an earthy contrast to the Beckford exotica. In the Duchess's bedroom there is elegant furniture by Hepplewhite and Chippendale. The dining room chairs are covered in Cordoba leather; fine silver candlesticks gleam on the seventeenth-century oak refectory table. Serving dishes are in the shapes of fish and game birds and there is even a wine decanter in the form of a Dodo!

Sporting paintings, sporting prints and trophies are everywhere; magnificent, intricately wrought ornamental silver enlivens every highly polished surface, there are strange silver gilt figures of ratcatchers and fur-hatted men crawling with animals, golden pomanders filled with aromatic spices to keep medieval smells away from sensitive aristocratic noses, a beautiful French satinwood table and fine eighteenth-century chairs in the Old Library. Beyond it is the most beautiful room in the house, the drawing room with its superb white and gold Italian ceiling, French furniture from the periods of Louis XVI and Louis Phillipe, Venetian looking glasses and Chinese porcelain. Above the piano in this room hangs a handsome portrait by Philip Laszlo of the donor of the castle. Mary Louise, Duchess of Montrose, a beautiful young woman of twenty-eight. The last Hamilton to live here, she added another treasure to Brodick's splendours — the garden.

There had been a walled garden immediately below the castle at its eastern end since the eighteenth century, formally laid out with herbaceous borders and colourfully planted beds. To this the Duchess added the woodland garden which runs below it to the shore, one of the finest collections of rhododendrons of all kinds from giants to dwarfs, a blazing display of myriad colours from April to mid-June, a pond garden, magnolias, calceolaria, gean trees and acacias and camelias.

Brodick Castle, in its uniquely splendid setting between the mountains and the sea, is a combination of all that is representative of the wide range of interests covered by the National Trust for Scotland. Its concern with the preservation of our national heritage lies not only in a fine aristocratic building stocked with wonderful man-made objects and flanked by a beautiful garden but in its relationship with a wild and untamed landscape of hill and water, moorland and shore — a true storehouse of Scottish splendour.

One of the Trust's most recent acquisitions in the Glasgow area is Blairvockie Farm, a 5,215-acre hill sheep farm near Rowardennan which incorporates one of the most evocative romantic names in the Scottish story, the 3,194 foot summit of Ben Lomond overlooking the largest freshwater loch in the British Isles, Loch Lomond, where the Lowlands meet the Highlands, the subject of one of the most famous ballads in the Scottish minstrelsy. *The Bonnie Bonnie Banks of Loch Lomond*, known and sung all over the world, is said to have been written by one of Bonnie Prince Charlie's supporters in Carlisle jail while awaiting execution. 'For ye'll tak the high road and I'll tak the low road and I'll be in Scotland afore ye' has moistened many an eye and sweetened many a dram down the years. For the next few, however, the task of the National Trust for Scotland is to 'tak' the low road' towards raising by public appeal the endowment fund of £350,000 needed to preserve and maintain this priceless landscape of Scottish heritage so that its rugged beauty can be enjoyed by all. Even landscape has to have a silver lining.

5

THE HIGHLANDS

NO MATTER what anyone says, the Highlands are different. Not just another mountainous region but a place apart. You can start into this ambience, atmosphere, sentimental re-association, anything you like from just about anywhere you like north of the far side of the Forth Road Bridge or on the road leaving Perth, past the St Johnstone football ground towards Pitlochry.

It is there, that wave of heather-induced nostalgia (perhaps stimulated by a pre-lunch single malt or a distantly heard piper or a snatch of the haunting tenor aria from *The Fair Maid of Perth*) as palpable as fair-fleshed perfume, a change of theme, an absurd veering towards Jacobitism, a blurring of the naturally acute political realism with historical sentiment.

In the north the National Trust for Scotland encompasses all facets of the Highlands and it includes two landmarks, Glenfinnan and Culloden, representing a period of just eight months, which fixed the Scottish Highlands in the world's romantic imagination forever — the Jacobite Rising of 1745, led by one of the most charismatic figures in any nation's history, Prince Charles Edward Stuart, the 'Bonnie Prince Charlie' of legend.

This rising, begun with only a handful of men landing on the west coast of Scotland from France, a bold, seemingly foolhardy, attempt to restore the exiled Stuarts to the throne of Britain, took the Jacobite cause — and many Highland clansmen — from high hope to disaster.

The 1745 Rising was the fourth and last attempt to restore the Stuarts to the throne. The first had foundered at Killiecrankie where Bonnie Dundee won a military victory but lost his life and, leaderless, the 1689 attempt fizzled out. The second in 1715 saw James II and VII, son of the brother of Charles II who had fled the country in 1688, in Scotland leading a rising which lost its impetus at the inconclusive battle of Sheriffmuir. There was an attempt with Spanish assistance to rekindle the fire of rebellion against the Hanoverian dynasty in 1719 but the main Spanish force never arrived in Britain and the three hundred Spaniards who were meant to provide a diversionary landing in the Highlands were easily defeated by General Wightman in a brief skirmish in Glen Shiel.

In passing, it is interesting to note that the weather was never kind to the Jacobites. The Old Pretender, the titular James III and VIII, was delayed by bad weather from landing in Scotland in time to play a significant part in what could have been the most telling Jacobite rising in 1715. In 1719 the main Spanish force, which was to have landed in England, was scattered by a violent storm and returned to base at Corunna, abandoning the invasion.

In February 1744, when 7,000 men under the command of Marshall Saxe were preparing to invade England, accompanied by Prince Charles, a fierce storm broke up the invasion fleet and drove the French transports ashore at Dunkirk with the loss of many lives. Ironically, Marshall Saxe then went off to the Netherlands where he defeated a mixed Hanoverian, British, Austrian and Dutch force commanded by the Duke of Cumberland — Culloden was the only battle Cumberland ever won. The weather at Culloden was atrocious, a gale of rain and sleet, and the starving Jacobite army was facing into it.

It was clear that foreign reinforcements were needed to ensure that a rising would have a real chance of success. James's son, Bonnie Prince Charlie, an impetuous young man of great charm, courage and determination, although dubious military ability, spent most of the years immediately preceding 1745 trying to raise support from the French who kept promising it but never delivered. In a fury of anger and frustration Charles sailed from Belle-Ile with two ships, the *Elisabeth* and the *Du Teillay*, on 16 July 1745 — destination Scotland.

With the now seemingly inevitable Jacobite luck, the *Elisabeth*, the escort ship carrying all the arms and 700 soldiers, was intercepted by a British man-of-war off the Lizard and, badly damaged in the ensuing fight, had to return to France.

Against all the wise advice offered, Charles insisted on going on and, with just a dozen men, landed on the island of Eriskay on 23 July to embark on what has been justly described as one of the most foolhardy enterprises in British history.

Advice in Scotland was the same as that given on the *Du Teillay* — go back and await a more favourable opportunity — but Charles was not to be thwarted. 'I am come home, sir,' the twenty-four-year-old Prince told his advisers, 'and I will entertain no notion of returning to that place from whence I came, for that I am persuaded my faithful Highlanders will stand by me.'

It is one of the most amazing examples of obstinate optimism in history but, despite the gloomy predictions with which he was faced on all sides, Prince Charles turned out to be right. The Highlanders stood by him till the end and suffered most grievously for it.

At Glenfinnan at the head of Loch Shiel on 19 August 1745, the Duke of Atholl

Mullach an Rathain.

unfurled the Royal Standard of the Stuarts, of red silk edged with blue and, James, Prince Charlie's father, was proclaimed King and Charles 'sole Regent of our kingdoms'. A manifesto was also read in which James made a number of promises to his subjects, among them that he would 'with all convenient speed call a free Parliament and free the Scots from all hardships and impositions which have been the consequences of the pretended union' and also that he would 'protect, secure and maintain all our Protestant subjects in the free exercise of their religion'.

Finally, the Prince himself addressed the gathering, exhorting the Highlanders in a moving speech, 'to be jealous of their own and their country's honour, to join with them in so glorious an enterprise with whose assistance and the protection of a just God . . . he did not doubt of bringing the affair to a happy issue'. The 1,300 men threw their bonnets in the air and their cheers echoed from the steep sides of Meall a Bhainne across the still waters of the loch.

The monument which marks this occasion stands at the head of Loch Shiel and was erected in 1815, a slim tapering tower built of coursed stone rubble standing about sixty-five feet high. The dramatic statue of a kilted soldier which stands on top was carved by the sculptor, John Greenshields, and was added in 1834. The statue is not meant to represent the Prince himself but is symbolic of all the men who fought and died for him and his cause.

On the wall round the tower there are plaques bearing the following inscription in Gaelic, Latin and English: 'On this spot, where Prince Charles Edward first raised his standard on the 19th day of August 1745, when he made the daring and romantic attempt to recover a throne lost by the imprudence of his ancestors, this column is erected by Alexander Macdonald Esq., of Glenaladale, to commemorate the generous zeal, the undaunted bravery, and the inviolable fidelity of his forefathers, and the rest of those who fought and bled in that arduous and unfortunate enterprise. This pillar is now, alas, also become the monument of its amiable and accomplished founder, who, before it was finished, died in Edinburgh, on the sixth day of January 1815, at the early age of twenty-eight years.'

The forefathers, to whom the inscription refers, were in it from the start. The Prince stayed at Glenaladale House the night before the raising of the standard at Glenfinnan and the Macdonald chieftain was with him for many months in his wanderings in the heather after Culloden.

At first, after Glenfinnan, the enterprise, referred to so glowingly by Prince Charlie in his speech below the Standard, seemed glorious indeed. It met with a success far greater than anyone but the constantly optimistic Prince had expected. Edinburgh fell and Prince Charles gave a great ball in the Palace of Holyroodhouse. The Government army under Sir John Cope was roundly defeated at Prestonpans, just south of the Scottish capital. The kilts and claymores poured over the border and struck as far south as Derby.

But the English Jacobites, apart from one regiment raised in Manchester, did not rally to the Stuart cause. There were desertions from the fickle clansmen who were keen to get back to their straths and glens. There were quarrels among the leaders. The Prince was for marching on to London, Lord George Murray, his most experienced general, was against it. Battles were fought at Penrith and at Falkirk but by then the Prince's army was in retreat. Finally, there was Culloden.

On the bleak moor beside Culloden House, on Wednesday 16 April 1746, the five thousand Highlanders and a few Irish and Scots mercenaries who had at last been released by Louis XV to fight with the Jacobites, faced nine thousand men

Falls of Glomach.

commanded by George II's youngest son, the Duke of Cumberland.

Again there was disagreement among the Jacobite leaders. Lord George Murray did not believe the moorland at Culloden was defensible; Prince Charlie disagreed. Cumberland was resting at Nairn with his well-equipped army, celebrating his twenty-fifth birthday, and the Prince's men decided on a night attack, hoping to surprise the Government army in unguarded revelry. Two miles from Cumberland's camp a drumbeat was heard, which convinced Murray that the enemy were on the alert and he gave the order to retire. The next day when battle was joined at Culloden at 1pm, many of the Jacobite army were still exhausted after their 20-mile night march and most of them had not eaten for twenty-four hours.

The battle lasted just an hour. The clansmen were mown down by Cumberland's artillery and charged manfully but uselessly through a merciless fire of musket balls and grape shot. Murray, although he had disagreed with the site chosen for the battle — and he was certainly right about that although his reasons for calling off the surprise night attack are more open to question — fought with great bravery and was one of the last to leave the field. Prince Charlie wanted to lead some of the survivors on one last charge but was virtually forced from the field. The odds were completely against the Highlanders — the usual Jacobite luck with the weather had sleet as well as grapeshot driving in their faces as they charged — but there were many instances of savage and reckless courage as if they knew they were fighting not only for the royal cause but for a way of life.

At Culloden The National Trust for Scotland, who have owned land around the clan graves and Old Leanach Cottage, one of the few buildings in the area which survived the battle and its aftermath, have extended their Culloden holding.

In 1981, with help from the Countryside Commission for Scotland and private benefactors, the Trust bought 108 acres of the battlefield from the Forestry Commission and cleared the area to give a more vivid impression of the ground as it was in 1746 and to provide a proper setting for the graves and the lichened stone memorials which were all that marked the site.

The road which had been constructed through the graves has been realigned and a new visitor centre was opened in July 1984 by Sir Donald Cameron of Lochiel, whose ancestor was one of Prince Charlie's chief supporters and who fought and was badly wounded at Culloden. The first Prince Charles in the royal family since Charles Edward Stuart, the present Prince of Wales, visited the centre in the month before it opened.

The new centre has full audio-visual facilities in the auditorium telling the story of the battle, the last fought on British soil. There is a study room with models and literature which can be used by school groups and other organised visits, a bookshop and a tearoom and toilets. Old Leanach Cottage, which served as a memorial battlefield museum, is now being restored to its original state when it was the farmhouse of the Leanach holding in the eighteenth century. The Trust launched an appeal for funds in March 1984 and grants have been promised or given by the Regional Development Fund, the Highlands Regional Council, the Highlands and Islands Development Board, the Countryside Commission for Scotland and the Scottish Development Agency among others, but more money is still needed. The address for donations and covenants is The Culloden International Appeal, The National Trust for Scotland, 5 Charlotte Square, Edinburgh EH2 4DU.

Bonnie Prince Charlie, after wandering for five months in the Highlands with a price of £30,000 on his head (which, it is the Highlanders' proud boast, nobody would claim), escaped to France on the frigate *L'Heureux* on 20 September 1746. Many historians and biographers have seized on the dissolute and wasteful life he led after his return to the continent until he died in Rome on 30 January 1788, but his conduct during his campaign in Britain — his charm, his courage, his cheerfulness in adversity, never better demonstrated than in the five months wanderings in the Highlands and islands of the north-west — were universally acknowledged and admired. It must have been hard to have the best days of your life when you are just twenty-four and he was sixty-seven when he died. Disappointment, disillusion are inevitable but to his last days he always showed a fierce and heartfelt affection for the Highlanders who had supported him and a real grief for what their loyalty and courage had cost them.

By contrast with the care and chivalry shown to the Government wounded and captured, by the Prince's express orders, after Sir John Cope's defeat at Prestonpans, Cumberland's follow-up to his victory at Culloden was the act of a barbarian. No mercy was shown on the field or off, even to Highlanders who had not fought with the Jacobite army or given it any support. Men, women and children were murdered and raped and their property ravaged and stolen. The Highland way of life was proscribed and the Government embarked on a vicious and brutal policy towards the Highlands that virtually amounted to genocide and which was still going on five years after Prince Charlie had sailed from Loch nan Uamh to France.

The aftermath of Culloden exacted penalties which were to leave a permanent scar on the Highands of Scotland in the deliberate extinction of the Celtic way of life — by killing, destruction, confiscation and deportation. A tragic time whose only compensation was to confer on the rugged landscape between Glenfinnan and Culloden an imperishable romanticism and a wealth of song and legend unequalled by any other period in Scottish history.

Some invading princes, however, having once arrived in Scotland, never went away.

One of the earliest was the Irish prince and warrior turned monk, St Columba.

Almost 1,200 years before Prince Charlie, he sailed northwards from the coast of Antrim and landed at the Port a' Churaich, the Port of the Coracle on the south coast of the island of Iona, just off the south-western tip of Mull.

Iona, just three and a half miles long by one and a half across had been a holy place for hundreds of years before Columba landed there in 563. There is something unique in the atmosphere of Iona, an openness to the sky above its rocky coast and low-lying hills, a quality of the light, a kind of unsavage quality rare in Scottish island seascape that makes it curiously apt for contemplation and devotion. The Druids are said to have had a temple there and on Dun Cul Bhuirg, at 332 feet the highest hill on the island, remains of a defensive wall and an Iron Age fort have been found in recent excavations.

But the recorded history of Iona begins at the steep, pebbly landfall in a bay protected by an offshore islet in the south of the island, now called The Port of the Coracle, after the frail bentwood and leather craft in which St Columba made his perilous voyage from Antrim.

Why did he come? Some evangelical zeal no doubt; Columba always had plenty of that fuelled by his early education at the monastic school at Moville and his studies at Clonard with the great St Finnian, to whom some of the finest scholars in Europe came for instruction in the arts and the faith. It is said that his voyage was made as a result of a vow taken before a battle he fought in Ireland against a prince who had violated the sanctity of his church; a vow to the Archangel Michael in which he promised that, should victory be his, he would depart from his native land and win as many souls for Christ as had been lost in the battle.

Why he chose Iona is not clear. It could have been a maritime accident —coracles are notoriously difficult to navigate — or it could have been a whisper from the past of the island's former reputation as a holy place of another religion. The early Christians were nearer the worshippers of pagan gods than later theologians and the Celtic monks had a predilection for settling in wild and lonely places. The tranquillity offered the right ambience for the contemplation of the relationship of the soul with God and the barrenness presented a physical challenge suitable to their austere concept of living and encouraged a proper holy humility.

Dr Samuel Johnson certainly felt there was something particular about the environment of Iona when he wrote after his visit there in 1773: 'We were now treading that illustrious island, which was once the luminary of the Caledonian regions, whence savage clans and roving barbarians derived the benefits of knowledge, and the blessings of religion. To abstract the mind from all local emotion would be impossible, if it were endeavoured, and would be foolish, if it were possible. Whatever withdraws us from the power of our senses; whatever makes the past, the distant or the future predominate over the present, advances us in the dignity of thinking beings. Far from me and from my friends, be such frigid philosophy as may conduct us indifferent and unmoved over any ground which has been dignified by wisdom, bravery or virtue. That man is little to be envied whose patriotism would not gain force upon the plain of Marathon or whose piety would not grow warmer among the ruins of Iona!'

No matter what was the island's history before the sixth century, Iona's fame and reputation now rest firmly on its status as one of the earliest Christian centres in Britain and on St Columba — converter of the Picts, defier of the Loch Ness Monster — he reputedly saved one of his monks from the beast's claws, warrior prince and implacable evangelist.

Unfortunately, little but conjectured stones remain of what Columba and his eleven disciples built on the island. Fierce pagan raids by the rapacious Norsemen destroyed such relics. The Abbey was gutted by the Vikings at least five times beteen 794 and 986, and many of the monks were killed, sixty-eight of them on the beach just south of the landing stage where the ferry comes in today from Fionnphort on Mull.

The raids were so devastating that at one time all the treasures were removed to Ireland for safe keeping — including, it is said, the famous Book of Kells, the illuminated copy of the Gospels, now in Trinity College, Dublin, and the shrine of gold and silver which contained the saint's bones.

In Reilig Oran — the graveyard of Oran, one of Columba's disciples, whom one grim tale says was buried alive at his own request as a sacrifice to the sanctity of the island — there are reputed to be sixty kings buried, forty-eight of them Scots, four Irish and eight Norwegian, among them Macbeth and his victim, Duncan.

Dr Johnson was somewhat sceptical of this attribution: 'Iona has long enjoyed,' he writes in his *Journey to the Western Islands of Scotland*, 'without any very credible attestation, the honour of being reputed the cemetery of the Scottish kings. It is not unlikely that, when the opinion of local sanctity was prevalent, the Chieftains of the Isles, and perhaps some of the Norwegian or Irish princes were reposited in this venerable enclosure. But by whom the subterranean vaults are peopled is now utterly unknown. The graves are very numerous, and some of them undoubtedly contain the remains of men who did not expect to be so soon forgotten.'

St Oran's Chapel is probably the oldest building on the island, other than the Iron Age fort on Dun Cul Bhuirg, but the tombs of the kings are no longer visible, although, in the museum next to the Cathedral, some magnificent examples of medieval tombstones of knights and noblemen, taken from the same site, are to be seen.

There were also the Black Stones of Iona on which the early Kings of the Isles took their coronation oaths and contracts of alliance, under the threat that perjury in such a sacred oath would turn the swearer black! Dr Johnson mentions the stones but did not see them, although legend insists that the Coronation Stone, now in Westminster Abbey is one of them.

The Benedictine Abbey, like the Nunnery nearer the village, is said to have been built by Reginald, son of Somerled, Lord of the Isles, but it has been extensively restored in the last two centuries.

Despite the often violent circumstances of its past, there is a strange air of peace about this holy isle. Some of the most striking emblems of the faith which it has always inspired are the stark, but often elaborately decorated Celtic crosses are outlined against the sea and skyline.

Perhaps, rather than Dr Johnson's portentous aphorism about patriotism and piety (which is inscribed on a bronze plaque on a wall on the road to the Abbey), Iona's best tribute as a complete place came from the composer, Felix Mendelssohn after his visit in 1829: 'When in some future time, I shall sit in a madly crowded assembly with music and dancing round me, and the wish arises to retire into the loneliest loneliness, I shall think of Iona.'

In 1979 a joint initiative by the Secretary of State for Scotland and the Hugh Fraser foundation made the National Trust for Scotland the owner of most of the island, in order to secure in perpetuity a seemly environment for the Abbey Church and the other sacred buildings which the Iona Cathedral Trust has administered since 1899. The Trust now owns all the island except for the Abbey and other sacred buildings and historic sites and a few other buildings bought from the Duke of Argyll before the Trust acquired the island.

Its concern is not only with the sacred sites, the historical relics and the conservation of the scenic beauty of the island, but with the lives and welfare of the one hundred or so inhabitants of Iona. The Trust has always felt very strongly that preservation without people is a sterile exercise and that a prosperous community is the best guarantee against neglect.

Even older than Columba and religion, Druidic or Christian, on Iona are the strange geological formations, the almost classical columnar structures found in the rocky faces of this region.

On the island of Staffa, just to the north of Iona, where such huge organpipe-like structures inspired Mendelssohn to write *Fingal's Cave*, the Hebrides Overture, are the best known examples of these rock forms. Staffa is not owned by the Trust but just across the sound, on the headland of Ardmeanach in the cliffs of The Burg on Mull itself, these formations are repeated as strange rock fossil trees, around 50 million years old.

This 1,525-acre stretch of wilderness, mountains and cliffs below the peak of Bearraich is one of the most splendid wild places owned by the National Trust for Scotland, kept in all its original savagery for the pleasures of the active with an eye for and a joy in rough country.

Iona.

And you have to be active, for the track to the fossil trees, set beyond two magnificent waterfalls feathering down from the high cliffs to the humped, uneven rocks bordering the sea, is rugged and narrow and often skirts perilously near precipice edges. It was made by goats and sheep, not man.

You have to clamber down a fifty-foot cliff to get on to the boulder-strewn beach to look at the fossil trees, strange impacted striations of rock in branched layers, accessible only at low tide.

Above, the five-hundred-foot cliffs rise steeply over the basalt columns to the machair which climbs the ben, the territory of the red deer and wild goats and sheep, with eagles and buzzards wheeling above.

The Burg was bequeathed to the Trust in 1932 by Mr A Campbell Blair of Dolgelly and is one of the most splendid pieces of wilderness in its care.

The remarkable variety of volcanic features along the sea cliffs; the eroded edges of a series of lava flows which poured down millions of years ago from a major group of volcanos in central Mull; the views from the cliff tops of the extraordinary basalt islands off the Mull coast, Staffa, Lunga and Bac Mor; the caves beyond the fossil trees and the great waterfalls together with the wildlife and the birds make it a rough unspoiled outpost of Scottish coastal land of exceptional fascination and challenge.

However, not all geology is to be learned on islands. In the village of Cromarty, on the north-east coast of Scotland, twenty miles north of Inverness on the tip of the Black Isle (despite its name, a peninsula between two firths and not an island) is the cottage where Hugh Miller was born.

It is small and unpretentious, and was acquired by the Trust in 1938 for its associations with Miller, geologist, writer and journalist and lay leader in the Free Church of Scotland, who was one of the outstanding Scotsmen of his time, in the early nineteenth century.

Miller was one of the most remarkable examples of that nineteenth-century Scottish phenomenon, 'the lad o' pairts'. The number of professors, doctors, writers and administrators who poured out of Scotland in that century, the products of humble homes but good village schooling, imbued by that thirst for knowledge which offered the only pathway to eminence for the underprivileged is a matter of well-authenticated legend.

Even among these, however, Hugh Miller was exceptional. He was a bit of a loner and it was his passion for the countryside, the coastline, the hills and the woodlands around Cromarty and the finds he made in the quarries in which he worked which eventually brought him fame, although his early ambitions had been literary rather than scientific.

Although his uncles offered to send him to college, but at the age of seventeen he elected to become a stonemason because, although the life was hard, he longed to work in the open air and also to have leisure in the winter months to pursue his studies in geology and letters.

It was during his fifteen years as a mason that he made many of the observations in quarries, mountains and sea shores which were to make his name as a geologist. But it was his writing which first changed the course of his life.

He began by writing an account of the herring fishing industry for the *Inverness Courier*, which also published some of his poems and in 1829 he published a selection of these under the title *Poems Written in the Leisure Hours of a Journeyman Mason*. It was not a great success but it did form the beginning of his friendship with Lydia Fraser, who later became his wife.

Because of his impending marriage, Miller abandoned stonemasonry and became, surprisingly, the accountant at the local branch of the Commercial Bank of Scotland after training in the south. This was to improve his social standing and make him more acceptable to Lydia's parents. He devoted his leisure to

The Burg, Mull, Fossil Tree.

Carlyle's Birthplace.

Robert the Bruce.

Souter Johnnie's Cottage.

Threave Castle.

Hugh Miller's Cottage.

continuing his writing and in 1835 published *Scenes and Legends of the North of Scotland*.

This book, a collection of the fast-dying folk tales of the north, was a success in its own right even although Miller, ever a searcher for intellectual or spiritual justification, sought to put his assembly of tales on a higher plane than mere ethnology or entertainment.

'Man in a savage state,' he says in his introduction, 'is the same animal everywhere, and his constructive powers, whether employed in the formation of a legendary story or of a battle-axe, seem to expatiate almost everywhere the same rugged track of invention.'

Hugh Miller's Cottage; his great-grandfather put his and his wife's initials above the fireplace.
(British Tourist Authority.)

Culzean Castle.

Culzean Guest Flat.

Culzean Castle.

His next publication made him one of the leading figures in the movement which culminated in the Disruption of the Church of Scotland, which sought to restore the right to choose the parish minister to the congregation, and take it from the laird. The laird's patronage had been eulogised in the General Assembly at Edinburgh and in a speech made in the House of Lords by Lord Brougham. A brilliantly written pamphlet by Hugh Miller, published in Edinburgh through the good offices of the manager of the Commercial Bank there, attacking this stance from the point of view of 'One of the Scotch People', brought him sudden widespread admiration and recognition.

As a result he was invited to Edinburgh to be editor of *The Witness*, the Evangelical Party's newspaper. He rapidly became a kenspeckle figure in the capital, with his shock of reddish hair, the checked shepherd's plaid worn around his shoulders over his rough tweed suit, and, as a journalist, a centre of religious controversy.

At first he found refuge from the strain and turmoil of the contention which broiled round his writing in his old love, geology. From a number of articles he published in *The Witness*, he compiled his most famous book, *The Old Red Sandstone* and later an autobiography, *My Schools and Schoolmasters*. But the clash between the geological evidence of creation as he saw it and the new theories being discussed about evolution (which were to be clarified in Charles Darwin's *On the Origin of Species by Means of Natural Selection*, published in 1859), the tug of faith against newly emergent scientific theory wore him out.

He was working on a new book, *The Testimony of the Rocks*, which was intended to tackle these problems from a Christian scientific viewpoint, when, on Christmas Eve, 1856 at the age of 54, tormented by doubts and illness, he shot himself.

The house in which he was born is the only one left of the old fishertown cottages of Cromarty. In the garden at the back is the sundial he made for the uncles who brought him up. His father was lost at sea when Miller was just five years old.

The thatched cottage was built by his great-grandfather, John Feddes, whose initials alongside those of his wife, Jean Gallie, are carved above the fireplace with the date the house was built, 1711. Feddes is reputed to have been a pirate and the cottage is said to have been built with his loot — Spanish gold.

Beside the fireplace is an exposed section of the original wall and, on the wooden staircase leading up to the room where he was born, Miller claims that, as a boy, he saw the ghost of his buccaneering great-grandfather 'steadfastly regarding me with apparent complacency'. In the birthroom is a scrubbed wooden chair on which Hugh was nursed.

Copies of the newspaper are in the next room, along with a display illustrating his geological, literary and evangelical work and letters from some of the most

Hugh Miller's Cottage, view of inside.

famous men of his day, including Charles Darwin, Thomas Carlyle and Thomas Chalmers.

In the geology room there are fossils of ancient armoured fishes from his collection, many of which he was the first to discover and which he wrote about in his book, *The Old Red Sandstone*. (The main collection is housed in the Royal Scottish Museum in Edinburgh.) All the captions to the specimens are taken from Miller's own notes on them.

This is an interesting house which, like many Trust properties, serves more than one purpose. It is a memorial to a remarkable man and also the last example of a kind of housing special to the area and now disappeared.

The Old Red Sandstone appears in its natural habitat on Beinn Eighe and Liathach, two mountains in the 16,100-acre Torridon estate transferred to the Trust through the National Land Fund in 1967.

The original estate came as part of the estate duty due after the death of the 4th Earl of Lovelace. After being accepted by the Inland Revenue, the procedures of the National Land Fund (which allows places of special interest to be purchased for the nation) transferred it to the care of the Trust. An additional 2,000 acres at Wester Alligin, west of the Torridon estate was given to the Trust in 1968 in memory of Sir Charles Blair Gordon and Lady Gordon, by their sons. With the

Fair Isle.

Church on Sanday.

Tenement House.

Beinn Eighe Nature Reserve to the east, owned by the Nature Conservancy Council but managed jointly for recreation and conservation, this is one of the finest tracts of mountain scenery in Scotland.

These are some of the oldest mountains in the world, once as high as the comparatively youthful Alps but worn away by glaciers, storms and other forms of erosion during 750 million years, to just over 3,000 feet. Their quartzite peaks, 150 million years younger than the mountains themselves, contain very early worm fossils, remains of some of the most ancient creatures who have left their traces on earth.

All over the north, the National Trust for Scotland provides thousands of acres for those people who are not afraid of the wind in their faces, of distance and height and muscle-stretching tramps over gnarled, rough-hewn ground; for students and observers of wildlife, birds, flora and fauna, deer and wildcats, birds of prey and the rare species of the empty, dramatic hillsides.

For people who are prepared to resort to the original and most primitive form of travel — walking — so as to be rewarded with special sights and scents and sounds. The heady perfume of bog myrtle, broom and heather; the roar of water falling from a great height; birdsong and the harsh bellowing of stags. But, above all, the incomparable views of the ever-changing hills — red at dawn and sunset, green and grey at noon, purple in summer, bronze in autumn and white in winter — there is great richness in such places, only available to those who leave the roads and strike out into the lonely hills.

You do not always have to go far off the road however.

At Corrieshalloch Gorge in Wester Ross, on the road from Inverness to Ullapool, there is one of the finest examples of a box canyon in Britain — a mile-long gorge, 200 feet deep and almost sheer, its width varying from 50 to 150 feet. The Falls of Measach plunge into it and in its dank depths trout swim in the deep pools and all kinds of unusual plants flourish — the lobe-leaved sanicle, many kinds of fern, spears of brown-flowered greater woodrush, woodmillet and mountain sorrel with wych elms, silver-barked birches, Norway maple and beeches clinging precariously to its banks.

Corrieshalloch is best viewed from the suspension bridge which crosses it. The bridge's safety is virtually guaranteed because it was built by Sir John Fowler, joint designer of the Forth Railway Bridge who once owned the estate of Braemore, in which the gorge is situated.

Further south, on the road to Kyle of Lochalsh, ferry port for the Isle of Skye, lie the Five Sisters of Kintail rising abruptly from Glen Shiel to heights of more than 3,000 feet, another of the most dramatic and beautiful mountain ranges in Britain. The Trust was able to purchase the 12,800 acres of Kintail in 1944 with a generous gift of £7,000 by the late P J H Unna, President of the Scottish Mountaineering Club. A great benefactor of the Trust, Unna appreciated as early

The Five Sisters of Kintail.

Greenbank: Glasgow.

Hutcheson's Hall: Glasgow.

Hill House.

as the 1930s that the new roads into the Highlands presented a threat to one of the last major tracts of wild and semi-wild land in Europe. He used his money and the resources of the Trust to try and ensure that the mountains and high moorland which he loved should remain inviolate to the motor-car and be retained for the pleasure of walkers who would respect their stark and untamed splendour.

The Kintail acres were added to the 2,200 acres of Glomach which had been given to the Trust three years earlier by Mrs E G Douglas of Killilan and the Hon Gerald Portman of Inverinate.

In the northern part of the Kintail estate, beyond the high range of the Five Sisters lies the 3,254-foot mass of Bein Fhada. On its slopes rises the Glomach Burn which flows northward to the River Elchaig and on its way tumbles over a cliff to create a waterfall more than twice the height of Niagara, although about three hundred times narrower and great deal more inaccessible.

The Falls of Glomach drop 350 feet into a fearsome S-shaped gorge, almost totally misted with spray when the burn is in spate. It is one of the highest waterfalls in Britain.

Like Torridon, Kintail and Glomach is deer country and care must be taken in the stalking season (approximately mid-August to mid-October). The deer are part of the local economy and the Trust is concerned to show at the Morvich visitor centre at the head of Loch Duich that stalking plays a more important part in local affairs than offering mere sport for the rich.

Lea MacNally, the ranger-naturalist at Torridon was originally a professional deer-stalker and now, as well as managing the 16,000-acre Torridon property for the National Trust for Scotland, on which roam four hundred red deer, he is the author of five books on Scottish wildlife, one of which won a Scottish Arts Council award, and one of the country's leading experts on red deer and eagles. Beside his house at the head of Loch Torridon, he has his own deer park and a deer museum.

But not all Trust properties in the Highlands are wild. Just 15 miles to the north of Torridon as the eagle flies (38 miles by road) lies Inverewe Garden, one of the most extraordinary horticultural achievements in the world. It is a garden of not only native but also very exotic plants — from Chile, South Africa, the Himalayas, New Zealand, the South Pacific and many other places.

Inverewe is on the same latitude as Siberia and Labrador and is the gift of the North Atlantic Drift — better known as the Gulf Stream — and a great deal of hard work inspired by its creator, Osgood Hanbury Mackenzie, who began it in 1862. Inverewe came into the care of the Trust in 1952, given by the daughter of Osgood Mackenzie, Mrs Mairi Sawyer to ensure the preservation of her father's life's work.

Over 100,000 people a year visit Inverewe — a year-long blaze of colour and fertility: rhododendrons, magnolias, flame flowers, Himalayan lilies and giant forget-me-nots from the Pacific, azaleas and orchids. There are 2,500 species in twenty-four acres of woodland on a promontory overlooking Loch Ewe and a scatter of small offshore islands.

There are islands much farther off-shore which are in the Trust's care. I have already mentioned St Kilda, Fair Isle and Canna in an earlier chapter, one virtually abandoned, one given renewal prosperity and one just recently acquired. What will become of Canna and its population of fifteen?

It is difficult to see just what role this outermost island of the Inner Hebrides has to fulfil. There is little accommodation for tourists apart from one letting cottage although the fine, sheltered harbour is popular with yachts during the summer. This protected anchorage between Sanday and the main island is also favoured by seals who will follow you ashore, Winnie Mackinnon, the Trust's young representative on the island told me, if you encourage them!

There is little possibility of development except on the traditional side of fishing although an experiment in oyster farming is in progress using modern methods of fish farming. So Canna is being preserved just to be itself for the people who live there now and the people who are prepared to make the long slow journey to get there. And that simple aim is no bad thing, for this island has much to offer the patient and discerning eye.

High on the hills, breaking through the green machair like the bones of the earth, are the same strange cliffs with their black basalt columns as on Staffa and the Burg on Mull. Great stretches of seascape with breathtaking views of the jagged stone peaks of the Cuillins on Skye to the north-east, the massive outline of Rhum to the east and the low purple shadow of South Uist, Eriskay and Barra on the western horizon give Canna an incomparable setting. The island's lifeblood is the farm where Iain Mackinnon grows grain and, with the help of his sons and daughters, rears magnificent long-horned Highland cattle, some of them of the rare, black-haired variety, as well as the inevitable sheep.

Canna is a beautiful island to explore and, apart from the scenery, there is plenty more to look at, something to rouse old ghosts and not a little to stimulate the imagination.

At the eastern end of the island is the ruin of an old tower on a sea-girt crag, An Coroghon, where one of the eighteenth-century Clanranald chiefs imprisoned either his wife or his Norwegian mistress (the story is rather vague as to the identity of the lady) who was giving him trouble. Another tale tells how the irate chieftain imprisoned the lady there to keep her from the amorous intentions of her lover, a Macleod from Skye. The story varies but the name of the rock means 'fetters', and it must have been a wild and desolate exile.

Only one of the three churches on the island is now used but at the western end of the island are three fascinating archaeological sites which take Canna's history back a long way beyond the sixteenth-century amours of the Clanranalds.

Below the great black cliffs on the southern coast, on a low-lying grassy

Glenfinnan.

Glenfinnan.

Ben Lomond.

terrace jutting into the sea is Sgor nam Ban-naomha (the Cliff of the Holy Women), a Cashel or Celtic type of monastery, said to be a nunnery dating back to the era of St Columba. It perfectly matches the propensity of the pioneers of the Celtic Church for selecting places conspicuously detached from the world for their settlements, for it is extraordinarily difficult of access by way of the steep cliffs and could only be reached from seaward in good weather. It is a site to be occupied by women only of high dedication and stamina.

This ear-shaped enclosure is to be seen clearly from the cliff-top: an outer wall with the shape of five other buildings distinctly marked within it, just a few rings and squares of pale grey stones now, above which the huge white-tailed sea eagles, the largest birds in the British skies, ride the winds.

A few years ago the sea eagle was as extinct in Scotland as St Columba's nuns, but they were reintroduced from Scandinavia to Rhum and some of them come over to hunt from the skies above Canna.

Halfway across the waist of the island, where it is narrowest, there are signs of an even earlier settlement, two earth houses with stone-built doorways on the southern slope of Beinn Tighe, possibly Iron Age dwellings and farther west by Garrisdale Point there are standing stones and hut circles and the remains of a fort. Beyond the earth homes, on the north-coast headland of Rubha Langanes, there are other enigmatically arranged groups of old stones, reputed to be the grave of a Viking king.

But not all belongs to the past. Across the wooden bridge to Sanday is the schoolhouse, where Sally Metcalfe, a bright English lass from Portsmouth teaches her three pupils — boys of nine, seven and five — to whom, among other things, she is giving lessons in Gaelic, keeping just a lesson or two ahead of the class herself!

Canna may yet prove to be one of the most challenging problems the National Trust for Scotland has had to face. On this remote island, the most westerly of the Small Isles, there was once a prosperous, self-supporting, agricultural community. The clearances, neglect and heightened social awareness effectively ended that, but since John Lorne Campbell took over the island in 1938 there has been a revival of corporate and working life on the island with increased planting of woodland and the introduction of a herd of pedigree Highland cattle. There exist a number of empty crofts which, if used properly, could enhance life and give a measure of greater prosperity to the island. But the future of Canna is a delicate matter and will test the resources and the imagination of the Trust to the full.

Such problems do not usually strike the public at large as lying within the province of the National Trust for Scotland whose image is too often one of a guardian of great houses, relics of the autocratic past which their owners can no longer afford to maintain. However, there are not too many of those in the

Highlands of Scotland — the savage aftermath of Culloden saw to that.

Within the area there is one noble house in the Trust's care which escaped the ravages of that brutal time, Brodie Castle in the Laigh of Moray on the east coast, 24 miles from Inverness.

The preservation of Brodie Castle was undoubtedly due to the fact that the Brodies managed to be on the right side in 1745. Alexander, 19th Brodie of Brodie, Lord Lyon King of Arms, the chief heraldic officer in Scotland, served with the Duke of Cumberland's army. However, having preserved his inheritance on the one hand he did his best to ruin it on another. In a letter to his brother, Alexander quoted the famous dictum from Sir Richard Bulstrade's *Miscellaneous Essays* published in 1715: 'There are four different Actors on the Theatres of Great Families; Beginner, Advancer, Continuer, Ruiner'.

Most such 'Actors' have fallen into one category, few have managed two. The 19th Brodie of Brodie, having saved his house and his lands by backing the Government and qualifying as a 'Continuer', died in 1754 leaving debts totalling £18,268 15s 4½d, an immense sum for those days, which left such a beggarly legacy that the estate had to be sold twenty years later. In addition to qualifying as a 'Continuer' and a 'Ruiner', there is a sense in which Alexander almost qualifies as an 'Advancer' too because the splendid eighteenth-century garden is the work of his time, although most of it seems to have been done by his wife, Mary Sleigh.

The Brodies are one of the most remarkable families in Scotland. Speculation among reputable historians traces the family back as far as the Pictish King Brude who was converted to Christianity by Saint Columba at the end of the sixth century. A more certain attribution is the endowment of the lands around the present castle to the Brodie family by Malcolm IV in 1160.

The present castle was built in 1567, as the mason's mark on the gable of the south-west tower attests, a typical tower house of the period built on a Z-plan with square towers set diagonally opposite each other.

The house was sacked by Lord Lewis Gordon in 1645, during Montrose's campaign to keep Charles I on the throne (the Brodies seem to have been entirely consistent in their opposition to the Stuarts!) and it had to be extensively rebuilt, although the original Z-plan seems to have been retained as the basis.

Since then the Brodie family, although enduring all kinds of trials and tribulations, making and losing fortunes, have managed to stay on the lands where they have lived for 800 years — there is still a Brodie there today in the private wing of the Castle, Ninian, 25th Brodie of Brodie.

Inside the splendid rooms and apartments, all kinds of treasures are on view. There are more than two hundred paintings, fine furniture, some splendid ceilings and a fascinating collection of historical bric-a-brac — swords belonging to Prince Charlie and Bonnie Dundee, (odd in such an anti-Jacobite house); a lantern said to have belonged to Guy Fawkes and the Coronation Robe of Queen Adelaide, wife of William IV.

The Hall of the Tenement House.

Brodick Castle.

Goatfell from the Display Room window in Brodick Castle.

Most of the contents came from the family of the last Duke of Gordon, who married a Brodie who became Queen Adelaide's Mistress of the Robes. He was the son of the famous Duchess who raised the Gordon Highlanders by offering the recruits kisses and shillings. A copy of Romney's portrait of her with her son, the last Duke who died childless, hangs in the drawing room.

The house is full of elaborately constructed French clocks and fine porcelain. In the dining room is an exquisite set of Chinese porcelain decorated with the family crest and the motto, 'Unite' — unfortunately, on two pieces misspelt 'Untie' by the Chinese calligrapher

Above the dining table is the most extraordinary ceiling in the house, magnificent or monstrous according to taste. A highly elaborate late seventeenth-century plaster ceiling, it is painted and grained to look like wood, with voluptuous figures at each corner, representing the four elements of earth, air, fire and water with a sensuousness which seems to belie the known characters of the 15th and 16th lairds of Brodie, in one of whose times it is presumed to have been created.

Both of them left behind personal diaries which chronicle the spiritual struggles, replete with dark Presbyterian soul searchings, of which this ceiling hardly seems an apt illustration.

The dining room is hung with family portraits, the earliest of which, a copy of the original by Allan Ramsay which was sold in hard times in the eighteenth century, is that of Alexander, 19th Brodie of Brodie who made such a notable bid to be 'Advancer', 'Continuer' and 'Ruiner' of the Brodie estates within his lifetime.

On the wall opposite the fireplace hang portraits of James, 21st Brodie of Brodie, painted by David Martin, and his wife, Lady Margaret Duff, in a fine portrait by Downman.

James eloped with Lady Margaret, daughter of the 1st Earl of Fife in 1767 and such an event can hardly ever have evoked a more civil comment than that of her brother, the 2nd Earl, who wrote, in a letter preserved in the castle: 'I am informed Mr Brodie and Lady Margaret have stole a marriage. I wonder neither one nor the other chose to drop me a little civil note. However that want of discretion gives me no pain. I wish they may pass a happy life together.'

Nor was this the full extent of his magnanimity. Seven years later, when the Brodie debts had become so heavy that the house was put up for sale, the Earl of Fife bought it and gave the ancient barony back to his sister and brother-in-law.

By no means are all the pictures in the beautiful rooms family portraits. On the main staircase is a striking Dutch canvas by Willem van der Vliet, dated 1626, *The Philosopher and his pupils*. There are Venetian scenes by Edward Pritchett and

Dining Room: Brodie Castle.

Liathach.

St Kilda.

Culloden: Old Leanach.

Culloden Moor.

James Holland and in the Picture Room there is a collection of modern paintings, including a fine Dufy, *Boats by a Pier* and a post-impressionist landscape, *Spring at Vaudreuil* by Gustave Loiseau.

Probably the most beautiful room in the Castle is the Drawing Room, part of the alterations and additions to the building made in the 1890s. It is a room of masterly proportions and design, a large room which manages to feel intimate. Not surprisingly it is the present Brodie of Brodie's favourite room.

But in the end the impression left by the properties held in trust by the National Trust for Scotland in the Highlands is not of the splendour of buildings nor the heritage of precious relics of our past but, overwhelmingly, of an incomparable and unique landscape, virtually untouched by man, with the deer moving on the mountain tops and the eagles soaring on the thermals in the blue sky — that sense of openness and space that only wilderness brings.

Boath Doocot.

Inverewe Peninsula.

Brodie Castle.

6

INVEREWE

FROM THE hill behind Inverewe you can see from Cape Wrath to Ardnamurchan on a clear day — and clear days are not the rarities here that some people would attribute to the west coast of Scotland. Inverewe is in the same latitude as Labrador and Leningrad — 58 degrees north, just 4 degrees south of the Arctic Circle — a lush and colourful garden on the wild west coast of northern Scotland, set on a peninsula where the winds howl in from the open Atlantic.

Sometimes, even the skill and foresight with which this remarkable garden was planned and created cannot totally withstand the winds. In 1982, the anemometer blew away at a wind-speed of 120-plus miles an hour and over two years Inverewe has lost more than 200 valuable windbreak trees. Yet for nine months of the year, the garden at Inverewe is alive with colour that is more tropical than Scottish, from an amazing display of plants and trees and flowers from all over the world.

Responsible for this horticultural miracle are two things, the North Atlantic Drift portion of the Gulf Stream which washes this coast and the dream of one man, Osgood Hanbury Mackenzie, born in 1842 in a chateau near the little town of Quimperle in Brittany — a chateau surrounded, remarkably enough, by Bluebeard's Forest, through which the Breton servants were afraid to pass at night because of fear of wolves.

This places the period accurately in its context. For things were very different then — wolves in Brittany, and down the shores of Loch Maree at the end of which lies Gairloch, Poolewe and Inverewe, there was no road and therefore no wheeled transport. Heavy goods which could not be transported on the back of a man, a woman or a horse were dragged across country on a kind of sledge with runners made from the adzed trunks of birch trees. Or they came in, as did much of the earth to form Inverewe Garden, by sea.

Osgood Mackenzie's father was the twelfth laird of Gairloch, who claimed direct descent from two kings, one Scots and one Norwegian, but Sir Francis died when Osgood was just a baby and he was brought up by his mother, a singularly strongminded and determined woman. It was she who bought the Inverewe peninsula for him when he was just twenty from the family.

In 1862, *Am Ploc Ard* — the High Lump, as the Inverewe peninsula was then known in Gaelic — was just as barren as the treeless hillside of Inverasdale across Loch Ewe is today. A neglected sheep farm, there was nothing on it but a small bush of dwarf willow, a rocky headland catching every wind that blew, constantly drenched with salt spray, with, apart from the low line of north Lewis forty miles away on the western horizon, nothing between it and Labrador.

What made this man who, according to his fascinating book, *A Hundred Years in the Highlands*, published just before his death in 1922, spent most of his waking hours killing things — birds, fish, deer, wildcats and so on; what made him try to make a garden in such an unlikely place?

The question is not easy to answer and Mackenzie himself makes little attempt to do so in his book which is mainly an account of his own sporting activities interspersed with tales of his ancestors, Highland customs and events and the habits of the various animals which he pursued. At the end there is a chapter on the Inverewe policies which gives some account of the garden. In it he says: 'I started work in the early spring of 1864 by running a fence across the neck of the peninsula from sea to sea, to keep out the sheep. I was very young then (not being of age when the place was bought), and perfectly ignorant of everything connected with forestry and gardening, having never had any permanent home, and having been brought up a great deal on the Continent; but I had all my life longed to begin gardening and planting, and had, I fully believe, inherited a love of trees and flowers from my father and grandfather.'

Osgood Mackenzie, apart from this brilliant streak of horticultural inspiration, seems to have been a typically arrogant and autocratic Highland laird of the period. He spoke French, English and Gaelic fluently and, in his early years, very much was under the thumb of his mother, Lady Mackenzie, 'a very domineering woman'.

There is an intriguing and not very pretty story about a curse on the family. Osgood Mackenzie and his mother had evicted an old woman, setting fire to her house because she could not pay the rent, and she was forced to move out with what was left of the roof. With this she made a sort of tent against the walls of the cemetery at Poolewe but the Mackenzies pursued her there and forced her to move on. The *cailleach* put a curse on them: 'I'm forced to live among the dead now but mark my words there'll never be a male heir at Inverewe while a Mary reigns.' Osgood's mother's name was Mary and his daughter's was the Gaelic version, Mairi. No male heir to the Mackenzies lived to maturity.

The other tale is less sinister but a little less authentic. Osgood Mackenzie saw an old man who worked in a bothy picking a clump of heather to make a broom, and said: 'That's my heather. You know that heather takes seven to twelve years to grow.' At least this showed a certain botanical interest.

The tenants on the Mackenzie estate had to give the laird so many days free labour each year and it was the crofters who carried the peat, and soil brought by boat from Ireland, up from the shore when the garden was started. It was a hard life and Osgood Mackenzie was a hard man, although probably no harder than many others of his time. But he created a small miracle, a garden on a lump of rock where all the soil had to be imported and fertilised with seaweed and a wise choice made of the plants, trees and shrubs which were to grow there.

Although in *A Hundred Years in the Highlands* Mackenzie bemoans the fact that he did not know when he started about species which might have made the struggle against the elements easier, strangely enough, in the gales which have swept the Inverewe peninsula since 1862, the plants and trees and shrubs which have stood up best to the blows of the wind and the fierce spear-thrusts of rain and sleet and the permeating contamination of salt have often been the non-native ones. The Corsican pines which form part of the shelter belt which protects the garden from the prevailing south-west wind were an early ally in Mackenzie's planning. 'They make nearly double the amount of timber compared with the Scots fir and are proof against cattle, sheep, deer and rabbit, which no other tree is that I know of,' he wrote.

Modern horticultural thinking, however, takes a different tack. Jim Gibson, the National Trust for Scotland's resident representative at Inverewe talked a few years ago about the effects of and remedies for recent gales. 'On the 2nd and 3rd of January when we were all recovering from Hogmanay to one degree or another, we had a 120-mile-an-hour gale from the north-west which arrived like an express train and left equally quickly after twelve hours. It knocked down 130 trees in the garden and about 200-plus in the forestry plantation to the east of the garden. Obviously our first priority was to get stuck in manually to salvage the garden and clear out what we could — getting the trees down, getting them away, some flat, some at an angle of 45 degrees, and to try to tidy up the damage sympathetically underneath, which is all hard work. No machines other than chain saws, just human muscle — lots of sympathy and much ingenuity.

'On January 17, 1983, we had a further gale from dead calm to dead calm in two and a half hours, with speeds up to 120 miles an hour. We had roofs off buildings, we had a tide, a high tide over the main road into the fields beyond and we had 60 trees down in the garden. The garden itself, all 64 acres, had lost 200 trees in one calendar year. The effect — to let in the wind. What we have had to do is to switch track entirely.

'Inverewe has been mainly Scots firs, Corsican pines, larch — those kinds of trees which Mr Osgood Mackenzie originally got from Colonel Grant of Rothiemurcus, who was a personal friend of his. Now today we feel that a tree that wears an umbrella in the winter, or a parasol is much more liable to blow down, bearing in mind it's got all its sails set. So what we plan to do is to go to beech, to oak, which were all here in history in this locale, nothofagus (a kind of beech from the Southern hemisphere), eucalyptus, sorbus all these kinds of plants. Quick grown, they don't mind shallow roots and will grab the red Torridon sandstone that we have to offer as an anchor. They are much more airy-fairy trees than a lovely Scotty or a lovely Corsican pine and also, the benefit is, of course, it gives us much more leaf mould which we've never had before at Inverewe. Good for everybody.'

Talking of the conditions on which Mrs Mairi Sawyer, Osgood Mackenzie's daughter handed over Inverewe to the National Trust for Scotland in 1952, Mr Gibson said: 'She made really two stipulations only. One was a very positive negative one and the other was a very positive one. She said she wanted her Inverewe always in the future to be open to the public. When she died, suddenly and tragically in 1953, she was getting about 3,000 visitors a year. Now we have from 110,000 to 118,000 visitors a year from all over the world. To that extent we are fulfilling her wishes. Her other wish which was most important was that she laid down absolutely no stipulations as to the well-being of her garden because, as a gardener, if you don't move with the times, whatever that may mean and be and do, the garden will simply go backwards. So she couldn't have given anybody a kinder and more thoughtful legacy.'

After Osgood Mackenzie built his fence across the peninsula of Torridon sandstone — the Torridon mountains can be seen in the background to the south — to keep out the deer and the sheep, on the seaward side he planted trees. They were mostly Scots firs and Corsican pines backed by hardwood trees and other conifers, and behind them the rhododendrons and other non-Highland plants for which Inverewe has since become famous. In places the red sandstone was left exposed and it is now planted with dwarf rhododendrons and heathers in the scree below with a Japanese hydrangea climbing the rocky face — typical of the way in which exotic foreign plants and native species intermingle happily at Inverewe.

In the Bambooselem enclosure — so-called because of its plantations of bamboo — there are handsome eucalyptus trees next to a larch up which climbs another brilliant Japanese hydrangea. Not far from a bed of Inverewe primulas is the astonishing Chinese Handkerchief Tree, so named because it produces strange papery handkerchief-like bracts. Hydrangeas and rhododendrons are very prominent but in the middle of the Bambooselem plantation is one of the most notable plants at Inverewe, the sixty-year-old and forty-foot-high *Magnolia Campbelli*, that strange tree which produces hundreds of large pink blooms, eight

Inverewe from the Walled Garden.

inches across, before there is a leaf on it.

Mrs Mairi Sawyer, Osgood Mackenzie's daughter who looked after Inverewe when its creator died in 1922, and handed it over to the Trust in 1952, used to say: 'Those horrible herbaceous borders people *will* try to make me admire in England! I hate banks of gaudy flowers jumbled together in what their owners call "glorious masses of colour".' She believed that plants needed and deserved elbow room and although there is plenty of colour at Inverewe — and much of it is glorious — it tends not to come in masses, but with every plant having its individual setting against a dark bush or trees or a row of shelter-belt tree trunks with the waters of Loch Ewe gleaming pewter-coloured between them.

Asked to write a Guide to the Gardens when the National Trust were taking them over, Mrs Sawyer said: 'What is the use of writing descriptions of gardens, when all the time plants are dying or being transplanted and new ones are taking their places?' Because a garden is a living and constantly renewable thing, descriptions are always in danger of being outdated. So if when you visit Inverewe you find things are not exactly as I have described them or in the places in which I have set them, remember it is the growth and death pattern of gardens which gives them so much variety. This account of Inverewe sets out to show what kind of garden this is — not specifically to act as a guide.

Although most of Inverewe has an only slightly tamed semi-wildness about it and the visitor does not move in orderly fashion from one neatly tended plot to the next, this woodland garden is, as it were, carefully orchestrated to give a series of impressions which seem entirely natural, although many of the components — like the eighty-foot tree hydrangeas — are in fact very rare.

The key is an amazing internationalism.

Around the Gate Lodges are Chilean crinodendrons and the pale purple daisies from the Chatham Islands to the east of New Zealand. As you walk up the drive there are heathers and tree heaths below the eucalyptus trees.

On the seaward side Chilean flame flowers spread over the clipped rhododendron hedge, while across the loch the bare hillside of Inverasdale reminds you of what Inverewe once was.

Past the house — built in 1936 after fire had destroyed the original house in 1914 — is the rock garden with all the traditional plants for this kind of setting: alpines , juniper, dwarf trees and shrubs; but also the extraordinary Poached Egg Plant from California.

Below the rock garden is another import from the Chatham Islands in the South Seas, the giant forget-me-not. When these plants were first brought to Inverewe, they were clearly having a struggle for existence. Then one day Mrs Sawyer read an article in *The Times* by a sailor who had recently been to the Chatham Islands and said he had been amazed to find plants growing there along the shoreline amid rotting seaweed and the carcases of dead sharks — and described the *myosotidium nobile*, the giant forget-me-nots. So she quickly bedded the ailing plants in seaweed from the shores of Loch Ewe and, in lieu of dead sharks, mulched them with pails of herring fry left behind by the tide. The plants flourished from then on.

An even more macabre piece of fertilisation was provided by a dead wild-cat, shot after preying on the Inverewe chickens, which she buried under a *buddleia asiatica* which had ceased to bloom and was three parts dead. It bore a profusion of blooms the next year and has never looked back since!

To the west of the house is a magnificent stand of trees — Californian redwoods, firs, and huge eucalyptus more than 100 feet high and a large Douglas fir, grown from a seedling which arrived at Inverewe by letter post a century ago.

In the Japan garden there are cherry trees and yellow poppy-like japonica,

Chusan palms and plants from Chile and the Canary Islands.

The trees which provide such necessary shelter at Inverewe sometimes suffer from the gales and have to be replaced judiciously, as we have seen, but even when they remain standing, as some like the magnificent Corsican pines have done for 123 years, they impose a certain pattern on the garden for, as well as shelter, they provide shade and shade dictates what kinds of plants can be grown.

Around the small pond and on the peat banks there are orchids from Madeira, blue Himalayan poppies and irises. The large pond has water lilies, hydrangeas, iris and primulas. At one time this pond was stocked with ornamental fish but that project was abandoned when the herons, which pose so elegantly on the rocks along the shore of Loch Ewe, ate them.

Along the Rhododendron Walk there are unusual and huge specimens of rhododendrons from all over the world, some more than thirty feet high, as well as primulas, meconopsis and American dogwood trees, the glory of the Carolina spring.

The Peace Plot, planted just after the First World War, is one of the more sheltered spots and among its treasures are the delicate and exotic rhododendrons of the scented *maddenii* species, whose perfume fills this corner of the gardens in the flowering months of April and May. In the America Plot below Bambooselem, on the way back towards the gates, are orchids, primulas and varieties of the pineapple family from Chilean Andes.

After the wild naturalness of the woodlands which make up most of Inverewe, the ordered formality of the Walled Garden comes as something of a shock. It was made by Osgood Mackenzie on an old strip of sea beach which was the only part of Inverewe free of rocks. Today it contains vegetables — many of them not grown elsewhere in the Highlands — a herb garden, fruit and flowers as well as a herbaceous border and shrub roses. The fruit and vegetables go to feed the staff and to provide the restaurant, on the path down to which typically, there is Moroccan broom and the spear-like New Zealand flax.

This then is Inverewe, an amazing garden for these parts in a most splendid West Highland setting with superb views from between its sheltering trees over the head of Loch Ewe to *Beinn Airidh Charr* above Loch Maree and the high peaks of the Torridon range to the south. The home of around 2,500 plants grown nowhere else in these latitudes, Inverewe is the gift of the Gulf Stream and the gardening genius of Osgood Hanbury Mackenzie and his daughter, Mairi, now perhaps the brightest and certainly the most colourful jewel in the crown of the National Trust properties in Scotland.

7

THE NORTH-EAST

THE GRAMPIAN region in the north-east of Scotland amply fulfils the popular image of the National Trust as being a custodian of stately homes. It probably has more castles to its undulating, river-threaded square miles than any other area in Britain and is orchestrated with a series of great names which resound like a clarion call of Scottish architectural splendour — Brodie, Craigievar, Crathes, Drum, Dunottar, Kildrummy, Huntly, Tolquhon, Corgarff, Braemar, Glenbuchat and the most famous, although by no means the most impressive of them all, Balmoral, the Queen's summer residence on Deeside.

Some of them like Glenbuchat, Huntly, Edzell, Balvenie, Kildrummy, Duffus, Tolqhon and Dunottar are ruins but many are still habitable and quite a few of those are now in the care of the Trust.

Dunottar, a natural fortress on a great sea-girt rock two miles south of Stonehaven has a particular place in history as the setting for one of the most dramatic episodes in the long and troubled history of the Honours of Scotland, the Scottish Crown Jewels. This regalia, one of the oldest in the world, consists of the Crown, which, tradition has it, is based on the original gold circlet with which Robert the Bruce was crowned at Scone in 1306, although it was remodelled by James V in 1540 with the addition of arches, enamel work and precious stones; the gilded silver Sceptre presented by the Pope to James IV in 1494; and the Sword of State, another papal gift to the same king in 1507.

They were sent to Dunottar for safety when Cromwell invaded Scotland in 1651, just after Charles II had been crowned with them at Scone and two years after the English Protector had destroyed the Regalia in London. The Castle was defended by George Ogilvie of Barras and when it became clear that it must fall, the Regalia was smuggled out by the local minister's wife, Christian Grainger, and buried below the pulpit in Kineff Church.

After his restoration in 1660, Charles II had the Honours disinterred and placed in Edinburgh Castle, but from the Union of the Parliaments in 1707 they remained in oblivion for more than a century. Sir Walter Scott 'rediscovered' them and they were put on public display in 1818 in the Crown Room of the Castle where they can be seen to this day.

Pre-fifteenth century, the Castles of Mar — so-called because they lie within the ancient Pictish kingdom of Mar — were built as much for defence as habitation but the later buildings were made less as fortresses than as symbols of wealth and authority, retaining in their design the battlemented features of an age when repelling an enemy was of prime concern.

The countryside around Aberdeen is full of great houses but it is rich not only in habitable stone monuments to wealth and power but also in cattle, farmland and the harvests of the North Sea from fish to oil. The nineteenth-century Earl of Aberdeen — known for his cultural pretensions as 'Athenian Aberdeen' —commissioned local artist, James Giles, to paint no fewer than 85 castles, and it was the sight of Giles' watercolours of Balmoral which persuaded Queen Victoria to buy the Decside castle as her Scottish home.

The River Dee with the Don are the waterways which bisect this territory. Known as 'the land of horn and corn,' it might perhaps more accurately be described as basing its prosperity on surf and turf for the wealth of this area comes from the richness of the farmland, which has made Aberdeen Angus cattle the greatest breeding stock in the world, and the produce hard-won from the steel-grey North Sea — trade with the Balkans and the western coasts of Europe, fishing and, more recently, oil.

The National Trust for Scotland does not own all the great houses but it has in its care some of the most splendid of them — Craigievar, Drum, Crathes, Castle Fraser, Fyvie, Haddo House and Leith Hall. Some of these were based on older structures but most of the Trust properties were built in their present form to say convincingly to all round 'Here is the seat of authority'.

An outstanding example of this is to be seen at Castle Fraser, just off the B993, three miles south of Kemnay and 16 miles west of Aberdeen, where a massive armorial table dominates the courtyard, with the Royal Arms of Scotland carved above the arms of the Frasers, who built and owned this castle and, below, the modest insignia of the mason, I. Bell, illustrating the pride which went into the construction of these imposing buildings.

Beneath the strawberry frieze in the Michael Tower — strawberries were the emblem of the Frasers, originally an Anjou family deriving their name from the French word for strawberries, 'fraises' — there is evidence of more gentle domestic virtues in the portraits (his by Faulkener and hers by Lawrence) of a handsome couple, Colonel Charles Mackenzie Fraser and his wife, Jane Hay. The story of their love is preserved in her letters in the Castle archives. Of his portrait she wrote: 'Your picture, for want of better, is very agreeable company, particularly so at breakfast when I am alone — but I wish it looked at me.' More bizarrely, the wooden leg he wore after he lost his own at the siege of Burgos in the Peninsular War, together with the bullets which nearly killed him, are preserved in the castle dining room.

As well as making these impressive buildings and their contents generally available to the public, the National Trust regularly make the Grampian castles come alive again in a different manner with concerts and recitals and special events for which they offer a setting of particular splendour and elegance.

Drum, near Peterculter on Deeside, is the oldest Grampian castle in the Trust's care. Its imposing square tower was built around the end of the thirteenth century, although the rest of the house is mainly Jacobean. For 653 years it was owned by one family, the Irvines, one of whom was the armour-bearer to King Robert the Bruce. In recognition of his services, Scotland's liberator king bestowed on William Irwin the Royal Forest of Drum in 1323 but there is a tradition that before Drum Castle the site held a hunting lodge made of timber belonging to the thirteenth-century monarch, Alexander III.

Alexander was a popular name with the Irvines — there were twelve generations of them. One was the hero of the nearby battlefield of Red Harlaw, where the men of Aberdeenshire defeated a wild bid for the throne by Donald, Lord of the Isles, in 1411, during the time when the Scottish king, James I, was a prisoner in England, writing his long poem, *The King's Quhair* to Lady Jane Beaufort who became his queen. Another Alexander, the ninth laird, built the seventeenth-century additions to the square tower, which form the castle as we see it today, an excellent and harmonious work of expansion, the corbelled turrets and crow-stepped gables blending handsomely with the ancient fortress.

Although the great medieval tower with its twelve-feet-thick walls is the most impressive part of Drum, the interior of the building has great charm. As well as the fascinating proportions of both the oldest and the Jacobean parts of the building, there are some fine family portraits by Raeburn and Reynolds, beautiful eighteenth-century furniture and porcelain from France and China.

Within 400 acres of grounds around Drum Castle, where there is still a remnant of the original Caledonian forest which once covered most of the north of Scotland and some of the old oaks from which the Aberdeen clipper ships were built, there run wayfaring trails and courses for orienteering, the new countryside sport which is a mixture of cross-country athletics and navigation. Here, the Trust provides facilities for these, as well as the gentler woodside walks and picnic places.

A lot of the maintenance and repair and improvement work done on these properties is carried out by volunteers, particularly young people who come from all over the country, partly to have a holiday in a particularly beautiful and

Drum Castle.

fascinating place but also to help to keep it that way. Ranger-Naturalist Karl Pipes has responsibility for the outdoor parts of Drum, Crathes and other Grampian properties, and he praises these young volunteers: 'We don't insist

Drum Castle.

they work, but we ask them if they will give us some voluntary assistance, doing
jobs such as cutting rhododendrons or planting trees, repairing footpaths — that
sort of thing. Actually, it's mostly the younger groups who seem to be the best

workers. They're very enthusiastic'. The work needed just would not be done without them, he explained. 'We are very dependent on it. We cannot afford to maintain properties as we'd like to maintain them, without voluntary assistance. One of the great things about the Trust recently is that we've got a group known as Youth in Trust who are all young members who do voluntary work. For example the wild garden at Crathes. They're renovating that. Doing a marvellous job.'

At Crathes Castle, three miles east of Banchory, another magnificent sixteenth-century tower house, built on land granted to another family who were adherents of Bruce in 1323, there is very considerable involvement with the community.

From the outside, Crathes is formidable and beautiful, another example of that domestic stone sculpture which flourished in the peaceful days after the turbulent times of Mary, Queen of Scots. The family who built the castle and lived here for almost 400 years were Anglo-Saxon — the Burnards, Burnats, Burnets or Burnetts, the spelling varies down the centuries — who moved north under the patronage of David I when Norman feudal rule grew too oppressive. First they settled in the Borders, where after 150 years of cross-frontier feuds and warfare, they became totally in sympathy with the cause of Scots independence and supporters of Robert the Bruce, who gave them lands in the less troubled and less vulnerable north in the Royal Forest of Drum in 1323.

It was the Burnetts of Leys, as they became known, who built Crathes, beginning in 1553 and taking almost the rest of the century to complete it. They were a family distinguished in other than the martial arts. In the sixteenth century one of the Laird's brothers entered the Church, two became eminent physicians and another Professor of Philosophy, making a European reputation for himself at Basle and the University of Montauban, north of Toulouse.

Sir Thomas Burnett, the seventeenth-century laird, was a friend of the great Marquis of Montrose, who stayed at Crathes in 1644 and spared the castle and its lands from the plunderous raids which his army exacted from Deeside on that campaign. Sir Thomas's nephew, Gilbert, became a celebrated Episcopalian churchman, Bishop of Salisbury and Royal Chaplain to Charles II, a prelate outspoken to the point of recklessness, who sent a famous letter to the king private — an epistle for which he was lucky to escape with only the loss of his Royal Chaplaincy! Gilbert's eldest son William became Governor of New York, New Jersey, Massachussetts and New Hampshire.

A nephew of Sir Thomas bought the lands of Monboddo near Strathaven and here in 1714 was born the famous or notorious Lord Monboddo, a judge of the Court of Session who was renowned for his belief in mermaids and satyrs and his firm conviction that men were descended from apes and born with tails which midwives conspired to cut off immediately after birth!

Lord Monboddo was visited by Dr Johnson on his way north for his tour of the Hebrides with James Boswell in 1773 and Robert Burns wrote two poems about his beautiful daughter, Elizabeth, an elegy on her tragically early death at the age of twenty-five and a paean of praise in his *Address to Edinburgh.*

> *Thy daughters bright thy walks adorn*
> *Gay as the gilded summer sky.*
> *Sweet as the dewy milk-white thorn*
> *Dear as the raptured thrill of joy!*
> *Fair Burnet strikes th' adoring eye*
> *Heaven's beauties on my fancy shine:*
> *I see the Sire of Love on high*
> *And own His works indeed divine!*

The Burnetts continued at Crathes up till 1951. The 11th Baronet emigrated to the United States of America in the nineteenth century and became a sheep farmer in Southern California on a large ranch of 25,000 acres, costing $3,000 when he bought it, but today of incalculable worth, including as it now does several towns, a race track, oil fields and factories, a university and Los Angeles airport.

Within the sturdy wall of Crathes Castle there are fine family portraits by the Aberdeen painter, George Jamesone, who studied under Rubens, and one of that intemperate moralist, Gilbert Burnett, Bishop of Salisbury, ascribed to Sir Peter Lely, the Dutch court painter knighted by Charles II. But the greatest treasure is the 'Horn of Leys', made of ivory, mounted with bands of gold and set with cabochons, a carbuncle and pieces of crystal, said to have been given to the Burnetts by Robert the Bruce as a symbol of their authority over the royal hunting forests. It hangs in a glass case over the fireplace in the High Hall. Then there are the superb, painted wooden ceilings, decorated with Muses and highly fanciful portraits of famous warriors like Alexander the Great, Julius Ceasar and Judas Maccabeus — most of them depicted in medieval armour — as well as improving mottos such as:

> *The slothful hand make the poore*
> *But the hand of the diligent maketh rich*

There is quite a lot of diligence in the grounds of Crathes Castle today. Regular volunteer groups keep the grounds in repair and make improvements. Down in the stables is the Base Camp, where the National Trust for Scotland has provided accommodation for parties of up to twenty-seven people who want to use the facilities available in the grounds of Crathes or help with Trust projects or a mixture of both.

Accommodation is simple but adequate. There is wood to be collected for the common room stove, a cooker, refrigerator and cooking equipment but the

Two armchairs, c. 1597 from Crathes Castle.

parties, mostly young people, bring everything else. The ways in which members of the groups who come here can help in the Trust's work include maintaining paths, clearing vegetation, doing woodwork and other building and painting. Recently a section of Army Cadets built a bridge across one of the streams which run through the grounds so as to make the woodland tracks more accessible. Most groups have a specific project of their own devising and combine that with working for the Trust.

A spectacle to rival that of the Castle itself is the garden — or rather gardens, for there are eight of them, created for the year-round display of fascinatingly different trees, shrubs and flowers. These brilliantly designed gardens are the work of this century — although the great dark yew hedges date from 1702 and suggest there was an earlier formal garden. They were made by Sir James and Lady Burnett, who gave the Castle to the Trust in 1951, a most fortunate and beautiful combination of his interest in trees and shrubs and her passion for herbaceous plants and design.

Each of the divisions has a theme. The Blue Garden, cerulean with myriad shades of blue. The Camel Garden with its two humps — white and yellow and pink. The Trough Garden with its mottled copper-barked tress and pink, red, orange and gold flowers. There are white borders with grey and silver foliage setting off the white flowers; the June Border is a mass of colour — lupins, iris, poppies and asphodel — dramatically set against the outline of the castle at one end and a doocot and at the other.

Above it is the Golden Garden, where the Trust's gardeners have achieved one of Lady Burnett's ambitions not accomplished in her lifetime. There is a Red Garden and a Rose Garden. The Pool Garden, all red, yellow and purple, is the most formally designed and the Fountain Garden shows infinite shades of blue encircling a Florentine statue. There is a quite remarkable diversity of plants, forming one of the finest collections in Scotland. Although there is something worth seeing at most times of year, the most colourful months are June, July and August.

The Great Garden of Pittmedden, another of the Trust's properties, on the A920, a mile to the west of the village of the same name and 14 miles north of Aberdeen on the road between Old Meldrum and Ellon, is the epitome of formalism. It was first created in 1675 by Sir Alexander Seton, who — as seems inevitable in this area — also had a connection with Robert the Bruce. One of his ancestors married the great king's sister and was executed by the English eight years before Bannockburn. His brother lived to be one of the signatories of Scotland's declaration of independence, the Declaration of Arbroath in 1320.

The inspiration for the garden originally came to Seton via his friend, Sir William Bruce of Balcaskie, a famous Scottish architect who rebuilt the Palace of Holyroodhouse in Edinburgh for Charles II in 1671 and who, on his visits to France, had greatly admired the chateau of Vaux-le-Vicomte built for Louis XIV's finance minister, Nicolas Fouquet by Le Vau, with large formal gardens by Le Notre. Bruce incorporated some of the garden ideas he had culled in France in his lay-out for Holyroodhouse and a noted cartographer, the Reverend James Gordon, minister of Rothiemay in Banffshire, produced an elaborate map of Edinburgh early in the seventeenth century, a 'Bird's Eye View' of the city and its gardens in detail which may have given Seton more ideas about laying out a garden in the French style in Aberdeenshire.

Today's Pitmedden Great Garden with its widespread lay-out gives the impression that these seventeenth-century designers must have visualised the gardens being seen from the air and in the original design a high retaining wall with viewing terraces to the north and south in part fulfilled this viewpoint.

When the Trust accepted the property in 1952 from Major James Keith CBE with an edowment for its future upkeep it was with the intention of recreating the Great Garden in its entirety. It was a considerable task, for by this time the three acres had become a kitchen garden and fires and other calamities had destroyed the old house that was replaced by a Victorian building which now serves as the Trust's headquarters for the Grampian area. The present design was evolved with the help of a committee headed by one of Scotland's great antiquarians, Dr James S Richardson, HRSA, formerly Inspector of Ancient Monuments in Scotland, helped by Lady Elphinstone and Lady Burnett one of the creators of the gardens at Crathes, and the Trust's adviser on gardens, Dr John M Cowan.

Appropriately, some of the design is patriotic, particularly one carrying the arms of its Seton founder, flanked by the Scottish emblems of the thistle and the saltire. The other three parterres or rectangular sections are taken from the drawings of Gordon of Rothiemay, following the seventeenth-century lay-out of the garden at the Palace of Holyroodhouse.

It takes 40,000 annual plants to maintain, create and repeat the formal patterns around the two fountains and twenty-seven sundials. The plants are raised in greenhouses and frames on the property and planted out in May within the three miles of boxwood hedges which form their borders. In the south-east corner the parterre bears the legend *Tempus Fugit* — 'Time Flies': not a bad motto for a gardener. The Great Garden is now the centre of a 100-acre property which includes a herb garden, fields containing a range of rare breeds of livestock and a Museum of Farming Life in Aberdeenshire.

Haddo House, four miles to the north of Pitmedden off the B999 road to Methlick, is very different from the Castles of Mar, these battlemented tower houses pointing like rockets at the sky. This is a building in the classical style of the great Italian architect, Palladio, created in 1732 by William Adam, the Edinburgh architect, father of the famous Adam brothers. Haddo was the home of the Earls and Marquesses of Aberdeen. The fourth Earl who was Queen Victoria's Prime Minister at the time of the Crimean War was a great improver and designer and the lay-out of the gardens round the house is largely his work, very much influenced by the great houses he had visited in England. But the avenue constructed in 1857 to commemorate Queen Victoria's visit to Haddo is a Scots mile — 220 yards longer than an English mile.

The Gordon family who became Earls and Marquesses of Aberdeen has a long and very complex lineage, incorporating, as well as several intricate strands of intermarriage, a wicked Earl who had at least four different establishments with separate menages, a link with the even more notorious poet, George Gordon, Lord Byron, and a record of more endearing eccentricities in addition to a long saga of public service and achievement.

William, the second Earl, was acquisitive. He married three times and by skilful negotiation managed to acquire at a knock-down price a substantial part of the estates of the Seton family (including the magnificent Castle of Fyvie, one of

Cylinder bureau, c. 1880 from Haddo House.

the National Trust for Scotland's more recently acquired properties) who had been attainted for their part in the 1689 Jacobite rebellion. By 1731 he had accumulated enough wealth to build a superb new house and it was he who commissioned William Adam to create Haddo in the Palladian manner on the site of the ancient family House of Kellie.

There have been alterations since but not many to the exterior view, and Haddo House remains a strange but elegant if slightly impractical building to find in Scotland's north-east. It represented the break with an older era, as Cosmo Gordon of Ellon wrote in his *Souvenir of Haddo:* 'Haddo belongs to the time when

Haddo House: North Corridor.

men recognized with relief that, even in Scotland, they could live safely in houses with large windows and airy rooms and could forget the tall fortress-like towers, many of which had been built in Aberdeenshire less than a century before. It is a house, not a castle, but when first built the new Haddo must have looked as modern to some of the neighbours as constructions of glass and steel look to us today.'

Inside, the rooms are partly classical, part Victorian — as in the ornate anteroom with its marble bust of Queen Victoria, the Drawing Room with its graceful proportions, spectacular chandelier and fine paintings, portraits of family and politicians by Sir Thomas Lawrence and others, landscapes by Giles, and the elegant library. A later addition is the chapel, designed by Sir George Street, architect of the London Law Courts, which contains a fine, stained-glass window by the pre-Raphaelite artist, Sir Edward Burne-Jones and a splendid organ built by Father Henry Willis.

The 7th Earl, who built the chapel, was Viceroy of Ireland twice and also Governor-General of Canada. He became the first Marquess, and he and his wife, Ishbel, were endearingly known as 'We Twa', the title of their joint autobiography, and flung themselves with energy and enthusiasm into all kinds of joint projects, from supporting Gladstone on his Midlothian campaign and carrying out the ceremonies of office in Canada and Ireland, to forming evening classes for farm girls and organising choirs.

On their return from Canada, they built an astonishing addition to their stately home, a wooden Canadian-style building beyond the south wing. It was opened by the American evangelists, Moody and Sankey, in 1890 but since that time has been put to more secular use. The hall was found to have excellent acoustic properties and in 1945, June, Dowager Marchioness of Aberdeen, herself a professional musician, founded the Haddo House Choral and Operatic Society with her husband, David.

Every year Haddo House has its own opera and music festival with stars like Janet Baker and an amazing repertoire which has included Verdi's *Macbeth* and Puccini's *Turandot*. So Haddo continues its association with the world of the arts. The rooms in which the brilliant 4th Earl, a distinguished man of letters as well as a politician, talked with his friend, the actor John Philip Kemble, still offer hospitality to theatre people and musicians.

All of the Grampian region has strong links with the sea — the 6th Earl of Aberdeen spent much of his life at sea to pay off the estate's debts and was eventually drowned after being swept overboard from a China-bound clipper off the coast of Nova Scotia — and the links with the sea and its trade and its produce are illustrated in one of the Trust's other properties, Provost Ross's House, the oldest surviving building in the City of Aberdeen, now housing the salty collection of Aberdeen Maritime Museum, illuminating the sea history of the

Provost Ross's House.

town and the district, from Balkan traders and fishing boats to gigantic oil-rigs.

The story of the sea in Aberdeen has many strands — building ships with wood and iron and steel; fishing with trawl and lines and drift nets; dredging out the modern harbour from the old shallow estuary; the harvesting of oil from whales and from beneath the North Sea.

In this old house, appropriately sited on Shiprow, the ancient cobbled road which was once the only route to the harbour, the home of the eighteenth-century Provost Ross, a merchant with considerable shipping interests, the age-long battle of man against the sea in north-east Scotland is illustrated and remembered, just above the basin where the modern oil-related ships serving the North Sea rigs moor and ply.

The North Sea played its part in the creation of what is widely regarded as the most perfect and the most dramatic of Grampian's castles, Craigievar, set on the Rock of Mar, 838 feet above sea level on the eastern slope of the hill of the same name on the A980, 6 miles south of Alford. In the fifteenth century the Craigievar lands belonged to the Mortimers and they are said to have begun building the castle towards the end of the sixteenth century. Like so many great families, though, they had money troubles, and in 1610 they sold the estate with the castle still unfinished to William Forbes, a younger brother of the famous Bishop Patrick Forbes of Aberdeen. The Mortimers might not have had so many financial difficulties had they been as bold about money as 'Danzig Willie', as the Aberdeen merchant who bought Craigievar was known for his dealings with the Baltic ports. When in difficulties, Willie borrowed money from his saintly brother who eventually wearied of being his banker and refused. Willie persisted, however, in his request for 1,000 merks, promising that adequate security would be provided. The Bishop agreed and Willie, when he called for the money and was asked who was the guarantor, said, 'God Almighty — I have none other to offer!' 'Well, brother,' said the Bishop, 'He is not to be rejected; you shall have the money. It is the first time such a security has been offered to me, but may God Almighty, your bondsman, prosper you and see that it does you good.'

Whether by this bold act of fiscal piety or other means, Willie prospered and became the apotheosis of the new type of Scottish laird, who was no longer a kind of medieval war lord but a man of commerce and peace who built and left to his descendants the most elegant and one of the most dramatic castles in Scotland.

Craigevar is tall. Six storeys of it seem to thrust skywards from the hillside like a great tree; its turrets and gables have an organic quality of line and mass matched by no other tower house. The first sight of it is breathtaking, yet as the eye becomes more accustomed to its shape and dimension, viewed from different aspects it constantly has more charms and angles of impressiveness.

Round Gate, Leith Hall.

In the interior decorations, particularly in the magnificent plaster work on the ceilings and the stucco cornices, the influence of the Renaissance is very strong. Yet despite its beauty and grandeur, the proportions are domestic. For all its elaboration and intricately wrought ornamentation this is a castle to be lived in, medieval in its shell conception, richly furnished and embellished, but a house, a place of peaceful pleasure, not a fortress. It is one of the finest buildings in Britain, not merely in Scotland — the supreme achievement of an architectural style which was virtually to die with it, unique and splendid in its setting, its realisation as a building and its interior style.

There are other good examples of domestic architecture in Grampian, notably Leith Hall, a mansion house on the B9002, a mile west of Kennethmont, which was the home of the Leith-Hay family from 1650 to 1945. Most of the Leith-Hays were soldiers and in their home are gathered the keepsakes and souvenirs of many campaigns, including items connected with Bonnie Prince Charlie (the Leiths and the Hays were staunch Jacobites) and their services in the Peninsular War, the Crimean and the campaigns in India and North America as well as homely treasures of silver, glass, porcelain and needlework and family portraits.

Leith Hall does not have the drama of the great castles like Craigievar, Crathes, Drum and Castle Fraser but it has its place in the north-east story and is well worth seeking out in its secluded position off the road between Rhynie and Huntly for its woodland gardens and countryside walks as well as the special qualities of the house and the interest of its contents.

New treasures in the north-east have been acquired lately in the massive and impressive form of Fyvie Castle, a stronghold dating from the thirteenth century, set on a natural mound on a bend of the River Ythan, halfway between Aberdeen and Banff on the A947. A royal castle in its earliest days — Alexander III granted a charter at Fyvie in 1222 — it has been owned by many great Scottish families, the Earl of Crawfurd, Sir Henry Preston, Lord Seton and the Gordons and Sir Andrew Forbes-Leith among them.

Much of the present building was extensively restored by the Gordons, the Earls of Aberdeen, who acquired it when the Setons were forced to flee the country for siding with the Jacobite cause with Bonnie Dundee at Killiecrankie. The second Earl bought it while he was building Haddo and it is fitting that the centrepiece of the splendid collection of paintings at Fyvie should be Pompeo Batoni's dramatic full-length portrait of Colonel William Gordon, swathed in tartan, set against a background of classical Rome. Most of the paintings, which include Dutch eighteenth-century masters, portraits by Gainsborough and Lawrence, Reynolds and Romney and an unrivalled collection of Raeburns, were acquired by Alexander Forbes-Leith, Lord Leith of Fyvie who made a fortune in steel in America at the end of the nineteenth century and bought Fyvie Castle, from whose former owners he claimed descent, in 1889 for £175,000. Sir Andrew

Forbes-Leith, Lord Leith's great-grandson sold Fyvie to the National Trust for Scotland in 1984.

Fyvie Castle.

8

TAYSIDE

FROM THE steep slopes of Ben Lawers, one of the highest mountains in Britain, towering above Loch Tay from which flows the famous salmon river of that name, to the windswept east coast towns huddled greyly against the icy eastern blasts from Russia and the Baltic and the glaciers of Scandinavia, to where the river runs into the North Sea, lies Tayside — at the very heart of Scotland.

Perth, the gateway to the Highlands, the city of Walter Scott's 'Fair Maid', was once the capital of Scotland, whose kings were crowned on the sacred stone, now in Westminster Abbey, in the nearby village of Scone. At one end of the River Tay, which winds most elegantly through the spires and crenellations of the Fair Maid's city, the scenery inland is wild and Highland; at the other end east coastal, low-lying and maritime, a region of contrasts of mountains, rich agriculture, beautiful gardens, battle-sites, lost causes and even two palaces.

One of those palaces is at Scone, formerly the Pictish capital and the site of the coronation of Scottish kings from Kenneth MacAlpin in 843 to Charles II in 1651. It is the home of the Earls of Mansfield and was largely rebuilt in 1803, although part of the sixteenth-century palace is included in the present building. The original abbey and palace at Scone were built by Alexander I around the beginning of the twelfth century and were destroyed by a Knox-aroused mob from Perth during the Reformation in 1559.

Ben Lawers on the north shore of Loch Tay is the central mountain in a range of five and is the highest mountain in Scotland south of Ben Nevis, just sixteen feet short of 4,000 feet. Most of the southern slopes of the mountain from about half a mile above the main lochside road to the summit ridge belong to the National Trust for Scotland. Here the main concern of the Trust is the care and conservation of a unique environment with a wealth of montane or Arctic-alpine flora.

In the Visitor Centre beside the road which leads over the pass Lairig an Lochan separating the Ben Lawers range from Meall nan Tarmachan range to the west, a low-lying building constructed so as to intrude as little as possible on the rugged landscape, there is a first introduction to the fascination and splendour of Ben Lawers. Displays depict the geological history of the mountain. Illustrated there too are the rare flowers and plants which are to be found on the mountain — pink campion, green and yellow cyphels, pale blue alpine forget-me-nots, mountain sorrel, the greenish-white Scottish asphodel, purple and yellow mountain pansies, a rich variety of ferns, lichens and mosses, plants from the Arctic tundra and the high Alps, mysteriously flourishing in Perthshire.

Various geographical and geological factors have contributed to the highly unusual and diverse flora of this mountain, including rainfall, temperature, wind, shelter and certain anomalies of drainage which have militated against the formations of large peat bogs on the southern slopes of Ben Lawers and its smaller neighbour, Beinn Ghlas. It is thought that these slopes were at one time largely covered in mixed woodland, probably of oak, birch and elm with willow and alder in the damper hollows, rowan and birch at the higher altitudes and pine on the drier patches of soil. The present vegetation on the lower slopes is the legacy of these forests modified by the felling of most of the trees and the grazing of sheep.

Many species growing on Ben Lawers' higher slopes are found in the European Arctic but some, like the mossy cyphel and the alpine forget-me-not, have more exotic distributions in the Alps, the Pyrenees and the Carpathians and similar species are found as far afield as the Caucasus, the Urals, the mountains of North and Central America and the Himalayas.

The centre also depicts the wildlife to be found in the area — buzzards, kestrels, sparrow-hawks and the occasional golden eagle. There are also red grouse, ptarmigan, curlews and skylarks, wheatears and meadow pipits; hedgehogs and moles, foxes, stoats and weasels, otters and wildcats; red and roe deer and the high-living blue or mountain hares which go white in the winter.

With all this information, however, goes a warning. David Mardon the Ranger at Ben Lawers National Nature Reserve and the Trust's man on the mountain, highlighted two of his main concerns — people and the place. 'It's a very high mountain,' he said, 'and on any high mountain in Scotland there are some risks with adverse climatic conditions which can be considerably more severe than at low altitudes. So it's advisable to take the precaution of dressing well for the hill in protective clothing because, even in summer, cold weather can occur. In particular, mountain boots are advisable because it's easy to turn an ankle on a rough stony path and you're quite a long way from help up there.'

He also spoke about the effect that people had on the place, the conflict between access and conservation. 'Really, the main clash is as a result of trampling on the hill. Some of the vegetation is severely damaged by trampling by the many thousands of feet that go up the hill. And the main problem is the scarring of the hill by these footpaths. The vegetation on the high mountain ridges is of considerable interest scientifically and it has been damaged by hill walking.

'The path problem was very evident when I came here and in one season I could see it worsening with erosion proceeding at a visible rate and the path widening. Many, many parts of the path had never been made up at all so it was just a strip of mud where the vegetation had been killed by trampling. Water running over it had begun to wash away the soil, and, once you have a muddy groove people no longer walk on it, especially in wet weather. They walk alongside and so you get a second path and then eventually a third and so on.

'So what we've tried to do is to fill in those muddy grooves with local stone, where possible, to provide a hard surface so there is no incentive for people to walk on the verge and the path remains at a narrow width. With a hardened surface it can take the wear and tear quite well.

'Ranger staff do some of the work but a great deal of the hard labour has been done with conservation volunteers. The British Trust for Conservation Volunteers and the Scottish Conservation Projects Trust organise teams of volunteers each year who come and carry out a large part of the really heavy work. We've achieved results with them that are aesthetically reasonably satisfactory. We consider the aesthetic qualities of the site very important so we have tried to preserve these as far as possible with the path work we've done.

'Obviously a man-made path looks to be a man-made path but the rocks and the turf we have repaired the verges with look almost natural.

The glory of being on a mountain top, the sense of space and isolation, gives the wilderness experience which the Trust's conservation of wild places like this has made possible. But the wilderness experience must be balanced between the number of people who want access to it and the ecology of the region. Visitor pressure must be contained with conservation needs so as not to destroy by over-use the very thing that brings people here. Not everyone agrees with the National Trust's policy about this. Rennie McOwan is a National Trust for Scotland member and a hill-walking enthusiast but he does feel that some of the principles which were an original part of the Trust's acquisition of some mountain properties are not being meticulously observed.

'The Trust had an outstanding benefactor,' said Mr McOwan, 'called Percy Unna, an Englishman of Danish extraction. And he either pioneered fundraising efforts to buy mountain properties or gave his own cash or his family's cash. Most of the mountain properties that the Trust have either come directly from him or indirectly through his inspiration. And he's particularly important today, I think, when everything is being — or there's a danger of everything being — controlled and developed, because he had a wild land philosophy. He wanted the mountains

Linn of Tummel.

in the Trust's care to have genuine wilderness quality. To be free from
development and free from artificial control of an ugly kind.

    'And that included things like no man-made paths. Hills were not to be made
easier and safer to climb. There were to be no man-made structures on the hills
and so on. Take the Visitor Centre. Some people feel there's nothing wrong with
the idea of a Visitor Centre but that it should be in Killin village. Because it is on
the mountain it breaks Unna's philosophy. And secondly, it attracts large
numbers of people on to sensitive ground and just as the case runs that if you have
a castle or a great house that has so many visitors that they start to destroy the
furnishings, the carpets and the *objets d'art*, the same applies to a mountain.

    'I can understand why people accuse people like myself of being elitist or selfish or loners who want the mountain to ourselves but that is genuinely not the case. Most of the people who are critics of the breaking of the Unna philosophy (including myself, if I might say so), give up quite a lot of their time to taking other people on the hills, particularly young people. And I am not denying access to the hills to anybody.

'What I am arguing is that the pattern should not be such that it starts to damage the hills, that people be drawn and directed into specific spots. I believe that to be a mistake. But the charge of elitism which is sometimes levelled, that people like myself are selfish, I believe to be unfair and unfounded. The real elitists are those who try to control where you will walk and where you will not walk'.

After, or perhaps with, man the most devastating destroyer of the environment on Ben Lawers is the sheep. The National Trust for Scotland has no real control over the numbers of sheep grazed on those hills because the tenant farmers retained their grazing rights when the property was bought in 1950 by the Trust's Mountainous Country Fund formed by the late Mr Percy J H Unna. 'The main enemies,' says the National Trust for Scotland on Ben Lawers, 'are sheep and human beings.' But, further down the Tay in Angus, sheep were not the enemy but the staple and mainstay of life.

The Angus Folk Museum in Glamis, housed in a row of five cottages given to the Trust by the Earl of Strathmore, provides instantly comprehensible physical evidence of a vanished world — the rural community of Angus in the seventeenth to nineteenth centuries. It was originally the work and inspiration of Lady Jean Maitland and it is an extraordinary and fascinating collection of the objects and implements, domestic utensils and artefacts which were the staple elements of rural life in Angus for the two hundred years which preceded the last war.

Until the Aberdeen-Angus breed of cattle, which is now one of the major beef-producing bloodstocks in the world, was developed at Keillor, near Coupar Angus in 1810, the old white-faced sheep, smaller and hardier than the black-face and with much finer wool, was the stock animal on which the Angus farmers and stockholders survived.

The Angus Folk Museum charts, accurately and vividly, a life that is gone —although some of it disappeared only decades ago rather than in the middle of the last century. It portrays not only the implements and associated objects of the working life but domestic objects and environments in which that life was lived. There are the dolls' houses, laboriously made by loving fathers or brothers, with which the little girls played; recreated too is a schoolroom of the period in which lessons were taught and learned and the kitchens where the family meals were cooked, with the iron ranges and spits which were such an innovation in their day. Here too is a reproduction with authentic furniture and fittings of the minister's parlour, with the schoolhouse, often the focal point of village life with its association with the special occasions, joyful and melancholy, of christenings, weddings and funerals.

There is a still-working loom in the museum where demonstrations of hand-weaving are given on one day each week by Allan Dale, who comes down from his private hand-linen producing business in Luthermuir to show that the old machine can still be put through its paces. The clattering linen loom saw a new prosperity come to Angus when the spinning and weaving of locally grown flax superseded the wool.

The clatter of the linen loom was a very familiar sound to the novelist and playwright, James Barrie, in the small house in which he was born in Kirriemuir, four and a half miles north of Glamis. His father was a handloom weaver and one of the downstairs rooms in the modest two-storeyed house in Brechin Street served as his workship. His youngest son turned out to be a weaver of spells.

Just a few months after Barrie's death in June 1937, Mr Duncan Elliot Alves of Bryn Bras Castle, Caernarvon, bought the house and the stone-built communal wash-house in the backyard which had been the boy Barrie's first theatre and presented them to the Trust with funds for their restoration. In Angus it is widely believed that but for Mr Alves's intervention the house would have been shipped stone by stone to America and the wash-house would be in Kensington Gardens in London, for projects were seemingly in hand for both moves by American and English admirers of the creator of *Peter Pan*. A friend of the Barrie family occupied the house until 1961 and restoration plans were shelved until that date.

Now the house has the desk, brought from Barrie's flat in Adelphi Terrace, London, where he created many of his famous characters, Peter Pan, Captain Hook, Mary Rose and The Admirable Crichton, together with Barrie's portrait by Sir John Lavery, his warrant of baronetcy and a number of original manuscripts. Here too are the *Peter Pan* costumes worn by two of the most famous actresses to play the role, Pauline Chase and Jean Forbes Robertson, and a complete collection of his books.

Kirriemuir served Barrie well as the background to many of his works. 'Thrums', the town of the handloom weavers featured in his first book, *Auld Licht Idylls*, published in 1888 after he had studied at Edinburgh University and worked on the *Nottingham Journal* before becoming a freelance writer in London in 1885. It was the background to many of his other works as well but it was after the success of *The Little Minister* in 1891 and its dramatisation in 1897 that he found his true metier, the theatre.

The horror of his brother's death when James Barrie was six and the effect it had on his mother remained with him all his life and from that grew the fantasy escapist never-grow-old world which he painted so brilliantly in *Peter Pan* and later in *Mary Rose* and *Dear Brutus*. In what is said to have been his first theatre, the wash-house in the backyard of the house in Brechin Street, he may have played out some of his first fantasies and for some of the smaller visitors to his birthplace, it still provides the greatest thrill of the excursion — a chance to come face to face with one of Barrie's most ominous characters, the crocodile in *Peter Pan* who swallowed an alarm clock.

The kind of enchantment which permeated many of Barrie's plays is found in a different form in another of the National Trust for Scotland's properties in this area. Branklyn Garden, on the north bank of the River Tay, just outside Perth, has been described as 'the finest two acres of private garden in the country'. A setting of flowering plants ranged most skilfully against multi-shaded trees, it was created on the site of a former orchard by the husband and wife team of John and Dorothy Renton. Mr Renton bequeathed it to the Trust in 1967.

There are plants from the Himalayas, China, Japan, New Zealand, Canada and Peru as well as native varieties; an outstanding collection beautifully laid out on a site whose restriction of size is made to be a bonus rather than a drawback. Most notable are the meconopsis, dwarf rhododendrons and alpines which attract visitors and botanists from all over the world. It is an oasis of peace and flowering splendour on Kinnoull Hill, above the turbulent River Tay and the roaring clangour of the lorry traffic running to and from the East Coast oilfields and the north along the Dundee Road just below.

At Dunkeld, farther up the Tay, we move from countryside, literary shrines and gardens in trust to another aspect of the work of the National Trust for Scotland which might be categorised, not unjustifiably, as 'people in trust'. The Trust owns twenty houses in Cathedral Street and High Street around a fine square leading to the ancient Cathedral. Most of these houses date from the rebuilding of the town after it was sacked by Bonnie Dundee's Jacobite forces as the aftermath to the Battle of Killiecrankie in 1689.

Dunkeld was an important ecclesiastical centre from early times, when Adamnan, Saint Columba's near-contemporary (628-704), biographer and the ninth bishop of Iona, built a monastery there. Saint Adamnan, as he later became, is a highly important figure in early literature because his *Life of St Columba* is one of the very few works to survive from the Dark Ages. Constantine, King of the Picts, built a larger church at Dunkeld at the beginning of the ninth century and in 850, Kenneth MacAlpin, first joint king of the Scots and Picts, brought relics of Saint Columba from Iona and established Dunkeld as the senior church of his kingdom.

However, by the middle of the present century, the Cathedral was in ruins, a victim partly of the appallingly destructive zeal of the Reformation and subsequent neglect. The modest little seventeenth-century houses surrounding it were also in decay. Today the Cathedral has been partially restored and a part of it is in use as the Parish Church. In 1954 when the Atholl Estates gave much of this property to the National Trust for Scotland, things took a turn for the better.

The Hermitage, Perthshire, picturesque folly, built in 1758.

Ben Lawers.

Falkland Palace.

Perth County Council also took a hand and when rehabilitation and restoration were completed in 1965, the Trust and the Council between them had rebuilt forty houses, let to private tenants who work actively in the town — in short, people who form a community.

There are also two shops. One is The Ell Shop, so-called because of the weaver's measure on the wall outside. Gillian Kelly, the National Trust representative for Dunkeld runs The Ell Shop. 'Most National Trust shops are attached to properties owned by the Trust,' said Mrs Kelly. 'Dunkeld is a bit unique because there's not one single large Trust property.

'Mostly we stock National Trust for Scotland lines. Some things are supplied direct from our warehouse and we also have things specially commissioned for us or designed by the Trust designer. We also buy in certain local craft lines —spurtles, horn goods, pottery, things like that.

'We opened the shop when we were really in a very perilous situation financially in Dunkeld. We were very keen to keep the Trust presence here because of our let houses and we were very confused as to what the future would be in Dunkeld. This shop had been let along with another one and when the lease expired we thought we would take a chance and open our own shop and see if that would improve the position for us. And it contributes quite successfully and substantially towards the deficit which was here before.'

If the first of the Jacobite hopes for the restoration of the Stuart line of kings died at Dunkeld in 1689, the second died near Falkland Palace in Fife in 1715. The last connection with royal use which this palace of the Stuart kings enjoyed was when Rob Roy Macgregor and his Highlanders occupied it before the Battle of Sheriffmuir, at which they fought in a vain attempt to put James Stuart, the Old Pretender, on the throne.

However, the Stuart kings and queens had a very real connection with Falkland. There was a castle here before the palace was built. It belonged to the Macduffs, the Thanes of Fife, the family who had the hereditary right to enthrone the kings of Scotland when they were crowned at Scone. In the garden of the palace, there are stonework remains of the thirteenth-century castle.

It was James II who first lived at Falkland and his grandson, James IV, the brilliantly talented Scottish king, who spoke seven languages and took a knowledgeable interest in everything from surgery to shipbuilding and who died tragically at Flodden in 1513, built the oldest parts of the palace at Falkland which are still to be seen today, He added the East and South Ranges to the North Range built by his father to complete the structure of a building occupying three sides of a square. The North Range was burned down in 1654 when Cromwell's troops were stationed at Falkland.

The South Range is the only part of the Palace which is in a good state of repair. James V added the facing of dressed stone to make one of the earliest

Soldier's Leap: Killiecrankie.

Glen Coe

examples of French Renaissance architecture in Britain, and to celebrate his second French marriage, to Mary of Guise, the mother of Mary, Queen of Scots.

This James had rather a chequered career with his French marriages. When he went to Paris to marry, by previous arrangement, the daughter of the Duke of Vendome in 1536, he so disliked the look of his bride-to-be that he refused to go through with the ceremony! Tactfully, the French king, Francois I, offered him one of his own daughters, Madeleine, in the place of the rejected bride and James and she were married on New Year's Day, 1537. But the Scottish climate proved too rough for the gentle Madeleine who died within two months of arriving in Scotland. James then opened negotiations for another French bride, whom he remembered from the court in Paris and who had recently been widowed. Thus Mary of Guise became Queen of Scotland.

Within the South Range is the only original interior which survives in Falkland, the magnificent Chapel Royal. It was begun by James IV and it is still in use today as a Roman Catholic Chapel. The beautifully carved oak screen is mostly original work dating from the sixteenth century (two of the whorled pillars were replaced in the nineteenth century) but much of the rest was skilfully restored when John Patrick Crichton Stuart, the third Marquess of Bute and Keeper of Falkland Palace, began his dedicated restoration of what remained of the Palace in 1887. There is a fine royal pew in carved oak, a beautiful set of seventeenth-century Flemish tapestries depicting the story of Joseph and Benjamin, a fifteenth-century panel of the Madonna and frescoes which

Falkland Palace: Library.

commemorate the visits here of Charles I and Charles II on the occasions of their coronations in Scotland.

The Scots Guards, whose colours now lie in the ante-chamber of the Chapel Royal were formed in 1642 and reassembled at Falkland in 1650 by Charles II, who presented colours to the Scots troops who guarded him, naming them his Scottish Life Guard of Foot. Charles came to Scotland to be crowned nine years before his coronation in England but his bid to regain his father's throne was thwarted by the defeat of his troops by Cromwell's Ironsides at Worcester and he had to flee to France, through a series of hairsbreadth escapes, after the battle was lost.

The father of the present Keeper of Falkland Palace, Ninian Crichton Stuart, served in the Scots Guards. Major Michael Crichton Stuart, MC, who fought in the Western Desert and served with the famous Long Range Desert Group in command of the Guards Patrol with which he made the longest patrol in military history — 4,000 miles behind enemy lines — commissioned the stained glass Scots Guards Memorial in the Chapel anteroom. In recognition of the regiment's long association with Falkland, Scots Guardsmen in uniform or wearing the badge of the Regimental Association are admitted to the Palace free.

The Crichton Stuart family trace their ancestry back to the same roots as the Stuart kings whose residence this was — the fourteenth-century Robert II. Incidentally, Falkland Palace still belongs to the Crown. The National Trust for Scotland is Deputy Keeper in perpetuity, responsible for the upkeep of the buildings and the surroundings gardens, helped by an endowment given by Major Crichton Stuart when the property was conveyed to the Trust in 1952.

In the East Range lies the superbly decorated King's Bed Chamber, largely rebuilt by the 3rd Marquess of Bute and finally completely restored by the Trust, a room splendid with imposing ornamentation and royal symbols and containing the magnificent carved gold bed of Brahan, of Dutch East Indies workmanship and dating from the reign of James VI. In the beautifully laid out garden is the Royal Tennis Court, the oldest in Britain, built for James V in 1539. Recent research has established that it is 86 years older than the court at Hampton Court Palace and the only one in the world still in existence of the *'jeu quarre'* type. The ancient game of 'royal' or 'real' tennis is still played here and there is an active playing group associated with the court. The tennis court is particularly appropriate because this was a place of relaxation and recreation for the eight Stuart monarchs who lived here, an escape from the cares of state, from enemies, and from over-zealous friends.

Literally, Falkland was once the happy hunting ground of Mary, Queen of Scots, and her parents, grandparents and ancestors. James V died here bemoaning the end of his dynasty — rather prematurely, for the Stuarts lasted until 1714 —but, curiously, the prime factor in their downfall, their adherence to the Roman Catholic faith, is still practised here, the only royal palace in Britain where this happens. The Stuart spirit still lingers among these ancient stones.

9

FIFE AND CENTRAL

THERE IS a real sense in which an important part of the work of the National Trust for Scotland is building bridges — bridges between the people of Scotland and anyone else interested and this land's architectural, historical and scenic heritage.

In Dollar Glen in Clackmannanshire, the smallest county in the centre of Scotland, the bridge-building is literal. The bridges built across the tributaries of the River Devon in the glen leading up to Castle Campbell in the Ochil Hills were reconstructed recently by the 75th Engineer Regiment as part of the Military Aid to the Civil Community scheme, just one of the many ways in which the Trust finds volunteers to help it work for everyone.

Burns once wrote a fine tuneful song about the River Devon:

> *Fairest maid on Devon banks*
> *Crystal Devon, winding Devon,*
> *Wilt thou lay that frown aside,*
> *And smile as thou wert wont to do?*

It seems unlikely that he was writing about this part of the River Devon, where the Burn of Care and the Burn of Sorrow plunge down precipitous ravines on either side of what was known as Castle Gloom, until its Campbell masters had its title changed in 1490. The castle was the principal lowland stronghold of the powerful MacCailean Mhor, the Earl of Argyll, chief of Clan Campbell, and it featured in quite a number of raids and skirmishes particularly at the time of the English Civil War, when the Earl of Montrose took the side of the king and his deadly rival Campbell of Argyll backed the Parliamentarians. Even today it is a sombre place, a fitting setting for the sermons of John Knox who is said to have preached there at one of the turning points of Scotland's history.

Glen Coe

Pitmedden.

Fyvie Castle.

Ten miles away to the south-west, across the meandering undulations of the River Forth, is one of the key places in the Scottish story. In 1931, the year after it was founded, the National Trust for Scotland spent the first £1,000 in its just created and exceedingly modest exchequer on acquiring the Borestone section of the battlefield of Bannockburn. By tradition this is the spot on which King Robert the Bruce established his command post for the battle which freed Scotland from English domination, fought over two days, June 23 and 24 in 1314.

Bruce had just 5,500 men, only 500 of them cavalry. Edward II, the English king had an army of almost 20,000. His objective was to relieve the siege on Stirling Castle because he believed if he could do so he would then have a base from which to win back all the lands which the English had lost in Scotland since Bruce had been crowned at Scone in 1306. At this time Scotland had no capital nor seat of government and Stirling Castle was of vital strategic importance because it commanded the centre of Scotland, the frontier between the Lowlands and the Highlands.

The Scottish King scored a stunning personal and morale-boosting victory before the battle began when, unarmoured, he was inspecting his troops and was charged by an English knight, Sir Henry de Bohun, whom he dispatched with one blow of his battle-axe. From that moment onward the outnumbered Scots never looked back. The Scots pushed the English back across the Bannock Burn; the English tried to outflank the Scottish army but were driven off by a diversion of spearmen under the Earl of Moray and fell back to spend the night in a weak position, near the Burn, tired and weary and dispirited after a long and unsuccessful day. Caught in an 'evil deep wet marsh' the next day and quarrelling among themselves about the leadership — the Earl of Gloucester challenged the right of the Earl of Hereford to command the vanguard and died an hour later on the Scottish pikes commanded by Bruce's brother, Sir Edward — they were uncertain and lacking in purpose. Their cavalry hurled itself, in successive broken squadrons, on the relentless porcupine-like schiltrons of the Scots pikemen who aimed for the horses and then despatched the riders with their swords and dirks. The English cavalry masked their bowmen in the rear from the Scots and as one chronicler recorded, the archers 'hit some few Scots in the breast but struck many more English in the back'. An attempt to get a body of archers into a more advantageous position was crushed by Sir Robert Keith with the Scottish light cavalry and in the centre the tide of spears bore the English knights back and was almost up to the English king, when an old knight, Sir Giles d'Argentine, hewed his way back to his monarch and led him from the field.

When the English sighted what they took to be another army on Coxett Hill, south of Stirling Castle on the Scottish left, they turned and fled. The second 'army' was only the grooms and camp-followers watching the battle from a safe distance but their presence on the skyline proved decisive and a great victory was won.

The Smiddy at Kippen as it was before Trust ownership.

Although much of that area over which the two-day Battle of Bannockburn was fought is now built over, the murals and audio-visual display inside the Visitor Centre give some idea of how the Scottish victory was gained. The Visitor Centre and Pilkington Jackson's thick-thewed bronze statue of the King redeem what is now a rather uninspiring site, hardly a fit memorial to that fierce spirit of independence in which the Scottish parliament six years *after* Bannockburn threatened to depose Bruce if he showed any sign of accepting English vassalage and which nobly trumpeted to the Pope in the 1320 Declaration of Arbroath; '*For, as long as but one hundred of us remain alive, we will in no least way be subject to the rule nor the domination of the English. In truth, it is not for glory, not riches, nor for honour that we fight but for freedom alone which no true man lays down but with his life.*'

Bannockburn was the culmination of Scotland's long and bitter struggle for independence and although the peace that was eventually signed with Edward's son, Edward III of England, in 1328 was an uneasy one, it did confirm and accept Scotland's right to its own King and to the autonomy for which she had battled with such fervour and courage.

Craigievar Castle.

Castle Fraser.

A rather differently independent Scots view was taken by the seventeenth-century Laird of Scotstarvit Tower in Fife, Sir John Scot, Lord Scotstarvit, a lawyer and a man of letters married to the sister of the poet, William Drummond of Hawthornden. He came into public life under James VI and died after Charles II's restoration in 1660 and was for a long time a Lord of Session and a Privy Councillor, a Covenanter who defied Charles I and a stout defender of the rights of the Scottish gentry against kings, nobles and commoners alike.

In the sixteenth-century Scotstarvit Tower, not far from Cupar, he wrote a singularly uninhibited series of biographical sketches of his contemporaries entitled *Scot of Scotstarvit's Staggering State of Scots Statesmen* which was not published until 84 years after his death. The kind of nebby individuality which he represented is a very real part of the Scots character and Sir John stood up for his rights — and those of a few other people — against kings, prelates and politicians, secure in his own concept of the law and his own 'guid conceit of himself'.

Sir John Scot founded the first Chair of Humanity at St Andrews University and this year to mark the 400th Anniversary of his birth and to honour the memory of this great man the University have decided to rename its Chair of Latin, the Scotstarvit Chair of Humanity.

The tower with its cap-house and rare conical stone roof is owned by the Trust and is under the guardianship of the Ancient Monuments section of the Scottish Development Department. Today it is deserted and echoing, a haggard stone relic of the past, although it can still be visited.

The real glories of the property lie a mile away across the A916 Cupar to Windygates road, one of the youngest houses in the Trust's possession, Hill of Tarvit, an Edwardian mansion designed for one of Dundee's jute princes. Its architect was Sir Robert Lorimer, the man responsible for the Scottish National War Memorial in Edinburgh Castle and the Thistle Chapel in St Giles Cathedral. Frederick Bower Sharp purchased the estate in 1904 and the present house was completed in 1906, it is not as remarkable as many houses in the Trust's care but a fine, luxurious house of the period. It was designed for Sharp and his wife and family not just as an elegant home but to provide a setting for their fine collection of paintings, furniture and *objets d'art*.

The magnificent central hall in carved and pannelled oak is constructed to be the frame for two superb sixteenth-century Flemish tapestries, one showing Alexander the Great receiving the mother, wife and children of Darius III of Persia after defeating him at the Battle of Gaugamela in 333BC and the other depicting a hunting scene chasing birds and boars with a moated chateau in the background. Also in this lofty but curiously intimate hall are some fine paintings of the Dutch school; Chinese vases and beautiful pieces of seventeenth and eighteenth century furniture in English and Scots oak and a parquetry bureau of the same period.

Next to the hall, the drawing room is a brilliant contrast, white walls and, an elaborate French style plaster ceiling. It was designed as a setting for Mr Sharp's impressive collection of French furniture but there are also some notable paintings — an Allan Ramsay, a Fantin-Latour and a Breughel among them. There is an antique Meshed rug in front of the fireplace and the elegant French furniture in kingswood and ormolu, mahogany and tulipwood was made by *maitres* who supplied the royal palaces of Louis XV and XVI. The *suite de salon* covered in Beauvais tapestry is Louis XVI and there are some excellent pieces of Chinese porcelain, Famille Verte eighteenth-century plates by K'ang Hsi; Famille Rose porcelain decorated with pink flowers by Chien Lung and a collection of Buddhistic lions, seated goddesses and vases in *blanc de Chine* from the late seventeenth century.

There is Chippendale and Regency furniture in the dining room, more Chinese porcelain and bronzes and another superb plaster ceiling with motifs of foliage and acorns and in another room — a second sitting room, once the smoking room — a profusely ornamented stone fireplace which came from Scotstarvit Tower and some interesting golf pictures. The Sharps were keen golfers and below the front lawn there was once a nine-hole private golf course. The pictures include some seventeenth-century Dutch scenes of golf on ice, some supporting evidence perhaps for the claim that golf began not in Scotland but in the Low Countries, which have golfing artifacts dating back to the eleventh century!

The main bedroom upstairs has the original 1905 Lorimer fireplace and most of the original electrical fittings, except for the central chandelier which is set in a dome. When you stand beneath it it produces an extraordinary echo effect —highly alarming the first time you experience it!

But there is a practical as well as decorative side to the Hill of Tarvit. During the winter a group of National Trust members meet here, all accomplished needlewomen, to repair and refurbish tapestries and cushions, carpets and banners for National Trust properties all over Scotland. Dorothy Robertson, a member of the group explained: 'It's purely a voluntary group made up of people who just want to do the work. They are all expert needlewomen but not qualified people necessarily and if we don't know how to do a thing we ask expert advice. We provide our own threads, needles and that sort of thing but the Trust do give us the actual material to work on. They bring the work to us — things that need doing.'

Among the many things which the group have remade or repaired to enhance properties all over Scotland are banners for Brodie Castle, curtains and chair covers for Kellie Castle, a tapestry for the Hill of Tarvit, a patchwork table cover for Hugh Miller's cottage in Cromarty, the kneelers for the Royal Chapel at Falkland Palace and three standards for the Scottish National War Memorial in Edinburgh Castle. 'We thoroughly enjoy it,' Dorothy Robertson said, 'although it does demand a lot of patience. But it's a hobby.'

Hill of Tarvit.

The first job this dedicated group of voluntary conservationists did for the National Trust was to repair a patchwork quilt for Kellie Castle, the ancient stronghold ten miles away to the south-east, whose old stones have other strong links with Hill of Tarvit. The father of the architect who built Hill of Tarvit, Sir Robert Lorimer, was the saviour of Kellie Castle.

There has been a castle here, a few miles to the north of the coast road round the East Neuk of Fife, since the days of Macbeth. Siward, Earl of Northumbria, led an army which invaded Scotland in 1054 during Macbeth's reign, probably to support a bid for the throne by Malcolm, the next Scottish king, whose mother was his kinsman. As such he appears in Shakespeare's play as the young

Malcolm's chief general. As a reward the Siward family were granted lands in Fife which they held until the time of David II at least, although there are references to Siward lairds of Kellie up to the time of Robert the Bruce.

From the Siwards the castle passed to the Oliphants — a record of an Oliphant marriage in 1573 is carved on the south face of the East Tower. Eventually, the Oliphants sold Kellie to Thomas Erskine, Viscount Fentoun, who killed the leader of the Gowrie Conspiracy in Perth in 1600, saving the life of his childhood friend and King, James VI. The grateful James made him first a Viscount, later a Knight of the Garter — an unusual honour for a Scottish nobleman — and finally Earl of Kellie. Although he died in London full of years and honours at the age of seventy-three he is buried in Pittenweem, just down the road from Kellie, where his gravestone can still be seen on the north wall of the Parish kirkyard.

There are Kellie coats of arms to be seen in the splendid plaster ceilings of the Dining Room and the Great Hall in the castle and the family managed to survive the turbulence of the 1745 Rebellion although the 5th Earl, Alexander, was a colonel in Prince Charlie's army and fought at Preston, Falkirk and Culloden.

Kellie Castle, Fife.

One of his sons, who subsequently secceeded to the title, Thomas, was a notable musician, a violinist and composer who directed the eighteenth-century forerunner of the Edinburgh Festival, the St Cecilia Concerts held in St Cecilia's Hall in the Cowgate in Edinburgh, a venue for events in the contemporary festival today.

Lack of heirs saw the castle fall into neglect and in 1829, on the death of the 10th Earl, ther was a 'muckle roup' when most of the contents of the house were sold and the castle was virtually abandoned.

At one time part of it was lived in by the manager of the local coal mine at Balcormo and the Great Hall was used as a granary by the tenants of the Home Farm. The whole place was gradually mouldering into complete decay by the middle of the nineteenth century and the only noteworthy event at Kellie in almost forty years was the birth, in the cottage east of the castle, of Archibald Constable, who was to found a famous publishing firm and produce the Waverley Novels of Sir Walter Scott.

In the building as it exists today, the oldest part is the fourteenth-century north tower. In the fifteenth and sixteenth centuries Kellie was extensively added to by joining up the old tower with two others, turning the Scots tradition of vertical building on its side. Thus it was when it caught the eye of James Allan Lorimer, Professor of Public and International Law at Edinburgh University, jurist and political philosopher who had formed the habit of holidaying in Fife where he found the fresh clear air of the East Neuk good for his asthma. He 'discovered' it on a family walk in 1877, a windowless and deserted near-ruin. The Lorimers fell in love with it and when the Professor found that the owner, the Earl of Mar and Kellie, was a co-trustee with him in the adoption of a French orphan, he persuaded the Earl to give him a long lease of Kellie of thirty-eight years, as an 'improving tenant'.

He and his family certainly turned out to be exactly that — as the latin motto above the door attests. It was composed by a colleague of Professor Lorimer's, Principal Grant of Edinburgh University, and in translation it reads: 'This mansion snatched from rooks and owls is dedicated to honest ease amidst labours.'

The restoration — or rather preservation because Professor Lorimer's aim was to keep Kellie as it was but made habitable — must have taken many more labours than hours of ease. The Earl of Kellie had undertaken to make the place wind and watertight but the family passion for creative improvement which seemed to imbue all the Lorimers arrived at Kellie Castle just in time. Louise, the Professor's youngest daughter gave this account of the state in which they found it: 'It was left to the rooks and the owls who built in its crumbling chimneys and dropped down piles of twigs which reached out into the rooms. Great holes let in the rain and snow through the roofs, many of the floors had become unsafe, every

Menstrie Castle.

pane of glass was broken, and swallows built in the coronets of the ceilings, while the ceilings themselves sagged and in some cases fell into the rooms . . . The garden, still encircled by a tumbledown wall, was a wilderness of neglected gooseberry bushes, gnarled apple trees and old world roses, which struggled through the weeds, summer after summer, with a sweet persistence.'

The talents of the Lorimers gave Kellie new life. Professor Lorimer's young wife, Hannah, was a gifted musician and a granddaughter of Robert Stodart who, with John Braidwood, developed the manufacture of pianofortes in the early nineteenth century. There is an 1825 Stodart piano in the Drawing Room. They had six children, all highly talented. Daughter Hannah was a musician like her mother but also painted, made models and carved wood, while John Henry became a famous painter. Some of his works are in the castle but others are in the Tate Gallery, the National Gallery of Scotland, the Victoria National Gallery in Melbourne and the the Louvre. Louise wrote ballads and remade the wild garden and the youngest, Robin, became Sir Robert Lorimer, the most famous architect in Scotland. After making over the castle to the National Trust for Scotland in 1970, Sir Robert's son, Hew Lorimer, the distinguished sculptor, still lives there.

It was through Hew Lorimer that Kellie Castle came to the Trust. He and his wife, Mary McLeod Wylie, took on the lease of the castle after their marriage in 1937, although most of the interior furnishings had been sold after the death of his

Castle Fraser.   *Drum Castle.*

Haddo House.

uncle, the painter John Henry, and they had to start from scratch to remake a home between the beautiful, elaborately ornamented plaster ceilings and the bare boards. Into this project Mary Lorimer, although a mother with three young children, poured all her energy and creative talent, refurbishing and recreating the living atmosphere of Kellie room by room, painting, embroidering, making and lining almost forty pairs of curtains to match the furniture from their Edinburgh home and other pieces bought to fit the Kellie image, and endlessly keeping fresh more than twenty flower arrangements all through the year from spring to autumn.

In 1948 the Lorimers bought the Castle and in 1970, after the death of his wife, Hew Lorimer sold Kellie to the National Trust for Scotland, who were enabled to purchase it by a grant from the Secretary of State for Scotland with his powers under the historic Buildings and Ancient Monuments Act, and through generous assistance from the Pilgrim Trust and an anonymous life member of the National Trust for Scotland towards the purchase price and the endowment of the property.

As in almost all the National Trust for Scotland properties, at certain times there are other things to do than simply look at what is there. Kellie has concerts and exhibitions and open garden days as well as housing a permanent exhibition in memory of the notable architect, Sir Robert Lorimer.

One of the places in the East Neuk of Fife which Professor Lorimer used to visit before he discovered Kellie Castle was the fishing village of Pittenweem, where one of his sons, the painter John Henry, bought and restored a seventeenth-century sea captain's house overlooking the harbour. This house is now the property of the National Trust for Scotland and let to a private tenant. It forms part of the Trust's Little Houses scheme which has already spent more than £3 million making habitable some of the smaller old houses in Scotland, many of them in fishing villages of Fife like Pittenweem, Crail, St Monans and Dysart; others in Culross, where the scheme began, in Dunkeld and Falkland and all over Scotland from Cromarty in the north to the Borders.

The Little House is generally a key example of the tradition of Scottish burghal architecture which goes back to the twelfth century, sometimes no more than a single storey 'but an' ben' and seldom having more than six rooms. It has stone walls — of granite, freestone or whinstone, and originally had a thatched roof but is now probably pantiled or slated. Often it will have an interesting ceiling, either panelled and painted or plastered.

The Trust's Little Houses policy is to encourage private owners, local authorities and other organisations to preserve the best Scottish vernacular architecture which can be lived in or put to some good use. In cases of particular environmental importance, the Trust itself will undertake the restoration and recover the cost in re-sale together with a reasonable profit. When circumstances

Kellie Castle, Fife.

dictate the building is sold to a buyer who employs either his own architect or invites the Trust to become his restoring agent. There are other options involving local authorities and preservation societies. In general, the purchaser enters into a conservation agreement with the Trust on terms agreeable to both parties and different in each individual case, not to alter the design or the use of the building without the Trust's consent and so as to ensure the preservation of the appearance and amenity of the house.

The actor, Paul Kermack, moved from a Georgian house in Edinburgh to one of the Little Houses in Crail in 1972. He had seen it originally as a ruin with a notice on it saying, 'This building is being restored by the National Trust for Scotland'. His house was built in 1712 for a Crail businessman called Robert Logan

Leith Hall.

St Abb's Head, Berwickshire.

Gray Mare's Tail.

and at one time it had been a farmhouse with stalls and byre alongside where the beasts were kept. Asked about the restrictions on owners of houses bought from the National Trust for Scotland, he said: 'The main restrictions are to do with the outside of the house. We are not allowed to alter that in any way. I mean, I can't paint murals on the end walls for instance. It has to stay more or less as it is now and it must be redecorated at least every five years or sooner if it needs it. But, apart from that, inside we're not allowed to make structural alterations though we can change rooms if we like and decorate just as we like. The only other trouble we've had is with the TV aerial. I wanted to put a TV aerial up at this end of the house, on that chimney stack there. But they said, "No, it would have to go on the other end" because then it would get lost among the other TV aerials. It would be rather nice to put up a porch at the back of the house because the winds tend to blow from the sea straight in the front door. But that would be taboo.'

What does it feel like living in a National Trust property?

'It's not open to the public or anything,' Paul Kermack said, 'it's a private dwelling, so it's just like any other house really. People come and peer at the front, occasionally at the plaque and at the lintels which say 1712 and 1718 but then everybody does that anyway. Crail has quite a few lintels and some of them go back to the sixteenth century.'

And selling the house?

'If we want to sell the house we have to offer it back to the Trust to begin with but that's merely a formality nowadays I think, because I don't think they would buy very many of these Little Houses back. They really want the money to restore others, you see. It usually goes on the market just like any other house.'

In Anstruther, just down the coast, there are not only more Little Houses but a highly important and fascinating museum housed in buildings which the Trust originally acquired and in which it retains an interest. The Scottish Fisheries Museum illustrates graphically and with a wealth of nautical material how the folk who lived in the Little Houses of the East Neuk of Fife did — and do — earn their living from the sea.

There are boats and nets in the yard outside; inside there are figureheads and fish in an aquarium, illustrating the kinds of catches the North Sea fishermen pursue. There are some very fine paintings of seamen and fisher lassies and boats; splendid pottery figures of fishermen and fishwives; and the wheelhouse of a modern fishing boat with all the contemporary electronic aids to navigation and fish-finding. Old navigation instruments are here too; models of boats of all kinds and showcases demonstrating different types of trawls and other gear.

The museum is housed in a curious collection of buildings round a courtyard overlooking the ancient harbour. One is a sixteenth-century Abbot's House because there used to be a chapel here for fishermen, which is a dependency of another Trust property, the Cistercian Abbey of Balmerino on Tayside — one of

Balmerino.

the few places in the care of the Trust which is now a ruin and which will remain one. Currently, it is just being made into a safer ruin to visit.

The prosperity of that other extraordinary cluster of small houses in the Trust's care in Central Scotland derived not from fish but from coal. Culross today seems an odd place for such an unglamorous activity for it looks like a film set — and is much used as one — with its marvellous backdrop of seventeenth and eighteenth-century houses. In fact, its original fame owes much to Glasgow's patron saint, St Mungo.

On the site of the ruins of the Chapel built to commemorate him in the sixteenth century, Mungo was born a thousand years earlier, the presumably illegitimate son of Thenew, a disgraced and banished Lothian princess who had

Dirleton Castle.

been cast adrift in an open boat at Aberlady to perish in the North Sea. The wind and tide brought her ashore farther up the Forth at Culross. In the sixth century Culross was already an important religious centre and one of the monks, St Serf, became Mungo's teacher. When his studies were completed, the young man travelled west to Clydeside where he founded a religious community of his own which eventually flourished into Glasgow.

He is buried in the crypt of Glasgow Cathedral, the only pre-Reformation Church of any size to survive unmutilated in southern Scotland, near the site of the first church. The city which he helped to found adopted him as its patron saint. In 1503, the first Archbishop of Glasgow, Robert Blackadder, built a chapel in Culross on the spot where Princess Thenew had come ashore. The ruins can still be seen today on the banks of the Forth to the east of the Burgh.

The monks who manned the Abbey at Culross were the first miners and the little town is honeycombed beneath its white-walled, red-pantiled, crowstepped, gabled and corbelled houses with the diggings of the delving monks and their successors. Their labours made Culross so important in the coal trade that a kind of hod — the Culross 'chalder' — became the standard Scottish measure for weighing coal. Salt panning was an offshoot of mining. Sea water from the Forth was run into large, shallow iron pans and evaporated over coal fires. At one time Culross had fifty salt pans. Coal was also an important factor in another Culross

Charlotte Square, Georgian House.

Georgian House: Kitchen.
(British Tourist Authority.)

industry — making baking girdles for cooking scones and oatcakes. Legend claims that the blacksmiths of Culross invented this celebrated Scottish kitchen utensil for Robert the Bruce so that his soldiers could bake their oatcakes, and for a long time the Culross girdlemakers had a monopoly of their craft.

The man who made most money out of the Culross coal — and its salt pans and its trade in girdles — was a descendant of the family of Robert the Bruce, Sir George Bruce, a friend of a later Scottish king, James VI, the first king of Scotland and England. Bruce's brother, Edward, had helped James towards the English throne and James approved of the family's energy and industry. He made Culross into a Royal Burgh with the right to trade with countries overseas. So the small ships of the time carried coal and salt and other exports from Scotland to the Low Countries and Scandinavia, often returning with a ballast of Memel Pine, the red pantiles which adorn the houses of Culross today.

Sir George was a great innovator and he tackled the mining industry at the point at which the monks had left off. The ancient miners had known there were thick coal seams running deep under the earth but they did not know how to drain and ventilate deep shafts so their mines stopped at thirty feet. With the 'Egyptian Wheel', operating thirty-six buckets on an endless chain using horses as power, Sir George made it possible for miners to work at depths up to 240 feet and went on to develop the Moat Pit, one of the mining wonders of the world in its time. A contemporary description echoes the astonishment of visitors at this feat: 'The miners followed the vein of the mine and in nine and twenty years they have digged more than one mile under the sea.' At this point a shaft led upwards above water level to a sea outlet, protected by thick, strong walls. At this exit from the mine, ships used to load coal without entering harbour and paying dues. However, one visitor's reaction was not amazement but alarm.

When King James VI visited the mine as a guest of Sir George Bruce in 1617 and emerged at the seaward end, finding himself surrounded by water he suspected yet another plot against his life and quickly raised a cry of 'Treason!' However he was rapidly reassured and led back to the fine house which Sir George had built for himself, known for its splendour to the townsfolk as 'The Palace'. Royalty did industrial tours even in those days.

When it came up for sale in 1932, the newly formed National Trust for Scotland bought The Palace for £700. It is a unique example of a merchant's house of the period with finely decorated walls and tempera paintings in a distinctive sixteenth-century domestic style — together with an iron door to the room where money and valuables were kept, also good merchant practice! Painted frescoes, many of them of an allegorical or improving nature predominate in the decoration.

Men's pleasures fond do promise only joys
But he that yields at length himself destroys

accompanied by a painting of a Siren, is a typical example. One in the 1611 building shows the Judgement of Solomon, said to have been a flattering gesture towards James VI who was fond of comparing himself with the Israeli king. No doubt the room was reserved for the royal visitor in 1617.

Sir George Bruce left his mark on the Palace — 'GB 1597' one on building and 'SGB 1611' on the other, for by the time he added the second building he was *Sir George Bruce*. He and his lady lie beneath an elaborate alabaster tomb in Culross Abbey, bizarrely surrounded by kneeling effigies of their eight children.

The purchase of the Palace encouraged the Trust to acquire other properties in Culross. The collapse of the coal industry in the eighteenth century and rock salt supplanting the more expensive and laborious process of panning, undermined the town's economy — like the tunnels beneath her walls. Even the famous Culross wrought-iron girdles on which Scotland had baked bannocks, scones and oatcakes for centuries were challenged and worsted by the new cheap cast-iron girdles made at the foundry at Carron, near Falkirk.

The poor condition of many of the old houses and the lack of rebuilding in Culross gave the Trust its chance. By the beginning of the Second World War the Trust owned more than twenty properties in Culross. One of them, The Study, the finest house in town after The Palace, with its crowstepped gables, the Outlook Tower — said to have been used by a visiting bishop — and its elaborate Norwegian-style painted wooden ceilings. The Trust paid £150 for it and nine other houses were bought for £168. Many of the buildings were absolutely derelict and a great deal of money had to be spent restoring them. Modern Culross, however, is a lively and broadly based community with thirty per cent of its population of just over 600 under twenty-four years of age.

So today, as well as film people and visitors, children come here on educational projects to sketch and learn what their country used to be like and to match in another piece of the pattern they can put into their ideas of what Scotland's future should be. In Culross, the National Trust for Scotland has recreated a town and helped to give it a purpose and pride in itself. Once again, it is a living community, a relic of the past and a factor in the present.

10

EDINBURGH AND THE SOUTH-EAST

EDINBURGH, a city between the hills and the sea, is the most visited town in Scotland. The Scottish capital is a constant reward to the eye with its fascinating buildings and constantly changing perspectives, medieval from the heights of the Castle Rock down the Royal Mile to the Palace of Holyroodhouse under the domestic mountain of Arthur's Seat; Georgian in its elegant eighteenth-century New Town with its squares and piazzas and symmetrical streets; and encompassing in Grange and Morningside and Newington some of the finest Victorian domestic architecture in Britain.

It is the home of one of the greatest international arts festivals in the world and the headquarters of the National Trust for Scotland. Edinburgh is unique —'the most extensive example of a Romantic Classical city in the world' as the *Pelican History of Art* calls it. In and around this splendid city the National Trust for Scotland has all kinds of properties, large and small, wild and ordered, reflecting the diverse characteristics of Edinburgh and the south-east of Scotland.

In November 1944 the House of the Binns became the first property taken into the care of the Trust under the Country House Scheme. This had been launched in 1942 and made it possible for the owner of a suitable house — that is one of special historical or architectural interest — to transfer it to the Trust with an endowment for its upkeep and to continue to live in it. The house belonged to the Dalyell family and is still lived in by Tam Dalyell MP and his wife, Kathleen, who is the Trust's representative for the Binns. It was presented solemnly on 30 April 1946 when the then thirteen-year-old Tam Dalyell gave the Earl of Weymss and March, deputy chairman of the Trust, a sod of earth from the land of The Binns, symbolising the gift of the property and the Charter which incorporates it.

'It was given,' Tam Dalyell says, 'by the conscious decision of my parents. In the 1930s they were wondering about the French *demeure historique*, then the war

The House of The Binns.

came. I was the only child, anything could have happened, and they thought that a place like The Binns really belonged to the nation rather than to an individual family. They didn't want to open it for what would have been seen at the time to have been their own money gain. Now, we may laugh at that all these years later but that's how it looked at the time and, therefore, when the National Trust approached them, they were very willing to give over the house and the land and it was the first country house that was given to the Trust.' Of the Dalyells' relationship with the Trust he said: 'We've had adult relations with the Trust all these years. I don't think there has been a cross word.'

'Binns' is another word for 'bens', the Scots word for hills and The House of the Binns is named for the twin hills overlooking the River Forth on whose western slope it is built. People have lived here for a long time. There is evidence of a Pictish fort on the hill behind the house and there is even a Pictish ghost — a little old man in a brown tunic seen gathering wood on the hillside.

The House of the Binns: Drawing Room.

The House, which is an amalgam of various architectural styles and modes, was begun in its present form by one of those Scots who took Dr Johnson's advice that 'the noblest prospect which a Scotchman ever sees, is the high road that leads him to England'. But Edinburgh butter merchant, Thomas Dalyell took that road a century before Sam Johnson was born, in the wake of James VI of Scotland and I of England. His father-in-law, Edward Bruce, first Baron Kinloss, was Master of the Rolls and one of two Scots selected by the king to go to England to negotiate with Robert Cecil, Earl of Salisbury, on the delicate matter of what would happen to the throne of England after the death of Queen Elizabeth.

When James succeeded to the English throne in 1603, Bruce went with him and so did his son-in-law, Thomas Dalyell, as Deputy Master of the Rolls. In London Thomas made his fortune and when he returned to Scotland in 1612, he bought the Binns and rebuilt the house into the basis of its present form. Fireplaces, ceilings and doorways, inside and out, reflect his pride in his new property where his initials intertwined with those of his wife, Janet Bruce, appear as a decorative and proprietorial *motif*.

His descendants added to the house; in the 1740s it was turned back to front as far as the main entrance is concerned and in the 1820s the east and west ranges were enlarged and battlements and crenellations added to make the House more impressive. Sir James, the 5th Baronet, who made these 'improvements' added another feature to the landscape when he built the tower on the hill behind the House with money won in an after-dinner wager. It cost £26.10s and a hundred years later the 9th Baronet installed a windmill in the tower to generate electricity.

Architecturally, the House of the Binns is principally a monument to 350 years of changing taste. The dormer windows on the south are almost all that remains externally of the 1622 building. The north entrance is eighteenth century and the crenellations and battlements, the rectangular hood moulds over the windows and the facade in general belong to an attempt at apeing the Robert Adam style, made in the 1820s.

Inside, the story of The Binns is dominated by one man, General Tam Dalyell, son of Thomas the butter merchant, a sinister and commanding figure in the troubled times of seventeenth-century Scotland. There was nothing buttery

The House of The Binns: Dining Room, refurbished 1972.

Malleny Gardens, 17th century house: Midlothian.

about General Tam. He took the side of the Royalists in the Civil War and, when Charles I was executed in 1649, he swore never to cut his hair or his beard until the Stuarts were restored to the throne. After Charles II's Scottish coronation in 1651 he became a major-general in the King's army but he was taken prisoner at the Battle of Worcester and thrown into the Tower of London — from which he is one of the few people ever to have escaped!

After wanderings on the continent, where, among other things, he reorganised the Russian army for Peter the Great's father, Czar Alexis Michaelovitch and fought against the Tartars, the Turks and the Poles, becoming a Noble of Russia and a general for the second time, he returned to Scotland. The wanderer's souvenirs — his Bible, sealskin-covered trunk, his beard comb, boots and Russian sword — are to be seen in the dining room. His 1611 Bible is one of the earliest written in Scots and because of a misprint of 'She' for 'He' in Ruth 3:15, is known as the great 'She' Bible.

It was the Bible which was to dominate the rest of General Tam's colourful life. Charles II put him in charge of the Royal task forces in Scotland after he was restored to the throne and his principal task was the supression of the Covenanters, 'the rebels in Scotland' as the king referred to them in a letter of commendation to General Tam after the battle of Rullion Green. He pursued the

Lamb's House: Leith.

Covenanters with such dedication and such severity that his enemies used to refer to him as 'Bluidy Tam' or the 'Bluidy Muscovite'. Sir Walter Scott vilified him as a monster in *Old Mortality* and among the many sinister activities attributed to General Tam was playing cards with the Devil.

The Devil usually won but one night Tam was the victor and Auld Nick was so enraged by this effrontery that he threw the table at him. Tam ducked and the table fell into the Sergeant's Pond, below the hill on the west. Rubbish, of course, but when in the very dry summer of 1878 the pond dried out, a heavy table of Carrara marble was found buried in the mud of the pond. You can see it today in the Laigh Hall.

General Tam was married four times — but never, despite his religious convictions, in Church! He died in 1681 and his widow, Marion Abercrombie, compiled an inventory of his possessions which offers a very different picture from the fierce, savage and bigoted soldier depicted by Sir Walter Scott — a pioneering gardener and arboculturist, a man of education and refinement, whose tastes had been richly formed by travel and who surrounded himself with fine things, emerges from the list of his possessions to set against the image of Bluidy Tam, the Muscovite. Which was the real Tam or were they two sides of one character formed by the strange and brutal times in which he lived? Certainly, the House of the Binns offers a portrait of a very remarkable man.

It is also the first muster ground of one of the most famous Scottish regiments, raised by General Tam himself, the Royal Scots Greys. When first raised it was known as the Royal Regiment of Scots Dragoons and it is said that the popular name came from General Tam having ordered 2,536 ells of grey cloth to make the Regiment's uniforms. During his service with the Russians, he had seen how effectively the Poles had used white as a comouflage in snow and he chose grey as the colour into which his troops would best fade into near-invisibility against the Scottish countryside. It is maintained in regimental history, however, that the grey uniforms did not survive General Tam. After his death they reverted to the usual scarlet. The name 'Greys' began to be used again only a couple of decades later when the Regiment was mounted only on grey horses. Even today, when they are amalgamated with the 3rd Carabiners to form the Royal Scots Dragoon Guards, the Greys keep their links with the House of the Binns.

Like the life of General Tam Dalyell and the history of the Scotland of his time, Priorwood Gardens in the Borders could be said to be dominated by religion — but here the domination is physical and picturesque not savage and bigoted. For Priorwood lies in the shadow of the red sandstone ruins of the Cistercian Abbey of Melrose, one of the Border Abbeys built by David I in the twelfth century and pillaged by almost every English raider from the fourteenth to the sixteenth century. Priorwood was originally part of the Abbey gardens and in its orchard walk there is what is virtually an apple museum. It follows the growth and

The Georgian House: Bedroom.

cultivation of the apple from those introduced by the Romans, like the Pomme d'Api, originally brought from the Peloponnese by Appius Claudius to Rome, through the apples which were part of the monastery gardens like the first named English apple, the Old Permain 1200, to the species which were brought in from Europe and elsewhere by travellers in the sixteenth to eighteenth centuries, like the Margil 1750. All the way to familiar modern varieties such as the American Golden Delicious and regional types such as the Melrose White, developed by the monks of the Abbey next door and the Flower of Kent, reputed to be the apple which fell on Isaac Newton's head in his mother's orchard and led to him unfolding the law of gravity. Blossom time in May is a particularly beautiful sight with the fresh, fragile pink flowers on the old trees set against the ancient outline of the Abbey.

However, there is a strong practical streak at Priorwood and in the National Trust shop near the gate you can buy a booklet called *A Taste of Apples* which offers splendid apple recipes, everything from drinks like lambswool (apples, ale, nutmeg, ginger and sugar) and apple tea to soups, casseroles, cakes and sauces.

But apples are not the most important thing at Priorwood. Here, for a change,

The Georgian House: Parlour.

the National Trust for Scotland which acquired Priorwood Garden in 1974, is concerned not with preserving the past but with conserving the ephemeral present, for Priorwood is one of the most important centres in Scotland for dried flowers. Many of them are grown in the borders of the garden and various methods are used in preserving them, ranging from drying in sand to preserving in glycerine or pressing.

Bettina, Lady Thomson is the inspiration behind Priorwood and its apples and its flowers. 'Well it really was dried flowers that we started with and the orchard has just been tagged on,' she says. 'We began in a very small way because we were just thinking of a new use for a Trust Garden. Then we found that people were very, very interested and we started selling in a corner of the shop and sold everything we produced. I couldn't believe that dried flowers would ever make so much money but eventually we decided to sell throughout the year instead of just having one sale. I prefer fresh flowers myself but I must say I have found that dried flowers can be very beautiful, I think particularly when they mellow. And there is economics of course. In winter, fresh flowers are frightfully expensive. With dried flowers you can have them there all the time.'

As well as selling the flowers which they grow and dry themselves, Priorwood also have a series of very useful leaflets, costing just a few pence, showing the different methods by which flowers can be dried — anything from the exotic blooms to weeds and herbs. A visit to the Garden, a look round the ancient Abbey and a stroll on the magical slopes of the Eildon Hills, where Thomas the Rhymer met the Queen of Elfland, make a very pleasant day out from Edinburgh.

Charlotte Square in Edinburgh where the National Trust for Scotland has its headquarters at number 5 is one of the finest Georgian squares in Britain and one of the glories of Edinburgh's eighteenth-century New Town, a piece of civic enterprise rarely matched elsewhere. The harmonious grouping of streets, crescents and squares to the north of Princes Street is called the New Town because it was one of the first examples of town planning, the dream of one of the Scottish capital's most enterprising and imaginative Lord Provosts, George Drummond, who in six terms of office between 1725 and 1764 did more to change the face of Edinburgh for the better than any man in the city's long history.

He was the moving spirit behind the scheme to drain the Nor Loch below the Castle and the long rocky spur of the Old Town, and build a new Edinburgh to the north of the old. The drainage of the loch began in 1759 and George Drummond himself, in his last period of office as Lord Provost, laid the foundation stone of the North Bridge in 1763 to link the old medieval town with the spacious fields of Bearford's Parks which had been bought by the Edinburgh City Fathers in 1716. An advertisement invited architects to submit plans for the New Town in 1766. There were six submissions and from them the Lord Provost and architect, John Adam, chose that of James Craig for a town on a gridiron plan, flanked by open-facing streets looking to the Castle and the Old Town on the south over the Forth to the hills of Fife in the north, with the axial street finishing in massive squares at either end.

One of these, at the western end is Charlotte Square, the north side of which is the work of the celebrated architect, Robert Adam. Behind the graceful Adam frontage to number 7 Charlotte Square, the Trust have not so much preserved as re-created The Georgian House, showing within the genuine period structure, the domestic framework in which a well-to-do Edinburgh family would have lived in the 1790s.

David Learmont, the Curator of the National Trust for Scotland and the man intimately and ultimately responsible for the realisation of projects of this kind, explained how it happened: 'Fifteen years ago or so, it didn't exist at all. Numbers 5, 6 and 7 Charlotte Square had passed to the National Trust on the death of the Fourth Marquess of Bute and Number 7 was probably one of the dullest interiors in the square. For many years, it had been the premises of Messrs. Whytock and Reid, very high-class antique dealers and furnishers, and when the lease fell in it was decided to display the house as a Georgian show house.'

A great deal of research went into discovering what this house was like at the end of the eighteenth and the beginning of the nineteenth centuries and a nationwide search was mounted in order to find furniture, furnishings and domestic objects which would make it an authentic house of the period when it was first lived in, was undertaken.

The Entrance Hall is hung with portraits by Reynolds and Raeburn and Dobson. A portrait of William Pitt the Younger hangs in the Inner Hall, where there is also a sedan chair, a form of transport which was popular in Edinburgh until the 1840s. The Dining Room is completely furnished in period — a Hepplewhite table set with a Wedgwood service, eighteenth-century wine glasses and two not such civilised items — round-ended knives which could be eaten from and, in the sideboard, a pewter chamber pot in which the gentlemen could relieve themselves after the ladies had retired! The table could be adapted to the number of dinner guests. At one time ladies used to sit on one side and gentlemen on the other. Later in the century came the modern practice of seating the sexes alternately, which was rather charmingly known as 'dining promiscuously'. The pair of dumb waiters in the Dining Room were used when the presence of servants was not desired. Gossip and scandal were the below-stairs currency of the day and especially juicy items were often sold from one house to another.

Between the Dining Room and the bedchamber is another domestic convenience of great modernity at the time, a portable, flushable water closet — a 'receiver' which still retains its maker's name and operating instructions. The bedroom is exceptionally handsome with its very fine four-post bed and original hangings. There are two drawing rooms, one full of paintings and chairs for formal occasions when the guests would 'promenade' and the back drawing-room or

The Georgian House: Kitchen.

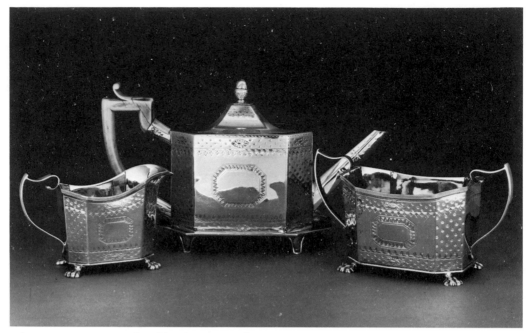

The Georgian House: Silver Tea Service, made in 1812-1813.

parlour, more cosy and intimate, which the family would use on a day-to-day basis. And, for their domestic entertainment, there is a barrel organ in a Sheraton-style case which plays a selection of Scottish airs.

The room which most visitors find particularly fascinating is the kitchen, painted blue, the traditional colour for keeping flies away. But it almost did not happen at all, as David Learmont explains: 'At the very first committee meeting when we were setting up The Georgian House, they didn't want a kitchen and said we would have a shop in the basement. I said we must have a Georgian kitchen; many things have only really changed in design in recent Visitors can see things that possibly they still have at home even today wereas they are not able to identify with formal rooms in the same way.'

So there, at his insistence, is an open fire-range, popular in Scotland until this century, a baking oven and a hot plate, all separately fired with hand-picked small coal; a copper *batterie de cuisine*, iron kettles and pots, pewter plates, earthenware and wooden vessels in the basement passage a china closet has recently been recreated with help from an 1826 inventory which referred to the contents and even a closet in Heriot Row.

If the Georgian House typifies the new elegant Edinburgh of the eighteenth century, Gladstone's Land in the Royal Mile, just below the Castle, exemplifies the more opulent end of the earlier era, the kind of thing from which the builders of the New Town were escaping. It dates from the sixteenth century, a typical tall building of the time, named after the merchant who bought it in 1617. It is arranged as a seventeenth-century merchant's house with a cloth merchant's booth on the ground floor and the first floor plenished as it might have been when the 1600s were fading into the 1700s. There are fine examples of contemporary painting on the ceilings and walls and a good collection of seventeenth-century furniture including some Scottish items. There is also an eighteenth-century panelled room. The second floor of the building has a modern use as a regularly changing gallery in the heart of Edinburgh for the exhibition of work by contemporary — today's contemporary — Scottish artists.

One of the chief joys of Edinburgh is that it has always been, in the best sense, an easy city to get out of. To the south lie the Pentland Hills and the Lammermuirs, to the east the Lothian coast and the North Sea, and to the north Fife and the road to the Highlands.

Fifty miles to the south at St Abb's Head, where the Lammermuirs meet the

St Abb's Head, Berwickshire.

North Sea there is wild country indeed. The Head, which became National Trust property in 1980 is the most important place in south-east Scotland for cliff-nesting seabirds and is a National Nature Reserve, managed in conjunction with the Scottish Wildlife Trust. More than 50,000 birds wheel and sail in the winds over the sheer cliffs rising 300 feet above the sea. The most numerous species are guillemots, kittiwakes and razorbills, with smaller numbers of shags and herring gulls and there are also a very few puffins. Gannets may be seen offshore, commuting between their fishing grounds and the Bass Rock, the granite volcanic rock which lies a mile and a half off Tantallon Castle on its sea-cliff coast near North Berwick.

Preston Mill.

Dirleton Castle.

In addition to birds St Abb's Head supports a wide range of plant species and several species of butterflies, including Grayling, Common Blue and Northern Brown Argus.

In 1983 the sea just offshore from St Abb's Head became Scotland's first voluntary Marine Nature Reserve. It has long attracted divers because of the exceptionally clear water and the spectacular underwater scenery with arches, gulleys and tunnels and a rich flora and fauna thirty to forty feet below the surface. The Ranger/Naturalist who runs St Abb's Head for the Trust said: 'People who've dived everywhere in the world from the Red Sea to the Bahamas, to the Barrier Reef all say that, given the weather, this has got to be one of the best dive sites in the world.' Asked why this should be, he replied: 'Two or three things. Firstly the water can be very clear. These cliffs drop straight down underwater to about forty or fifty feet in places so the underwater scenery is as spectacular as on land. Secondly, we have a mixing of waters here, coming around from the Atlantic and down from the Arctic, so there's a diversity of marine life down there from two different water movements. For example, there are a variety of different anemones and you get startling contrasts from the two different marine streams, like a Cup anemone from the south-west living alongside a great big ugly fish called a wolf eel which comes from the Arctic.'

Just twenty miles up the road nearer Edinburgh, water, this time fresh water, was a vital element in the prosperity of the region. At Preston Mill near East Linton the National Trust has in its care one of the oldest and most attractive working water mills in Britain.

Until water was harnessed to drive the mill wheel to grind the corn, barley or oats, the excessively tedious and exhausting business of making grain into something resembling flour by grinding it between two stones was woman's work, done laboriously by hand. The power generated by running water has been known for at least 2,000 years. By 1660 the picturesque mill at Preston, East Linton, was quite a sophisticated piece of machinery, using the power of the River Tyne to drive a wheel which links through a series of cogs to crush the grain, dried over the kiln fire. The dried grain is sieved, 'cockled' in a revolving drum to throw out weeds, carried up in small buckets on an endless belt and passed between the shelling stones, sieved again and winnowed with a fan blowing away the chaff and fed into the grinding stones from a hopper. The grinding stones can be adjusted to give coarse, pinhead, medium or fine oatmeal. All done by water power in a highly ingenious gearing system which has been in use since the days of the Romans.

Preston Mill, in its beautiful setting by the river with trees and the lush meadows of Lothian around it, the pantiled roof, the coned kiln and the huge

Phantassie Doocot.

mill-wheel slowly turning, is highly picturesque and has attracted generations of painters and photographers. It has also been extremely fortunate in attracting a wealthy and knowledgeable sponsor.

When the Mill came to the National Trust for Scotland in 1950 from the estate of Mr G B Gray, there was also some money which began a fund for its restoration, because, by the end of the Second World War, both buildings and machinery were in a serious state of disrepair. There was help from local tradesmen with skilled labour but the machinery continued to deteriorate and in the 1960s Preston Mill was adopted by one of the largest and most modern milling organisations in Europe, Messrs Rank Hovis McDougall Ltd, whose founder, Joseph Rank, had begun his career a century before in a similar small, wind-powered mill in Hull. Directed by experienced members of the Rank staff, the old mill was put back into working order and it still works today, so that the 9,000 visitors a year who go to Preston Mill can see how grain has been milled on the Tyne for centuries.

Not far from Preston Mill with its marvellously paintable outline, with its pantiled roofs the very spectacle of old-world charm, there is another building, Phantassie Doocot, a large conical structure with a cut-off roof, pleasing and unusual enough in shape but an unhappy neighbour for a grain mill. This, a couple of hundred years ago, was home for 500 pigeons, kept to supplement the laird's winter meat ration when meat from other sources was scarce or unavailable, the pigeons not caring (as the laird didn't) whose grain they ate to fatten themselves for the landlord's table.

Doocots (dovecotes in English) were introduced to Britain by the Normans although their origin is Roman, the *columbarium*, some of them of incredible sophistication, with automatic feeding and running water for baths as well as drinking. The Roman *penchant* for exotic engineering extended even to pigeon houses. The French copied the Romans in this, as in much else, with their *colombiers*, built in a profusion of architectural styles, and it is even said that doocots were a factor in the French Revolution because tenant or peasant farmers had to look on impotently while the landlord's pigeons ravaged their crops. As Phil Sked's excellent booklet on Preston Mill and the Phantassie Doocot points out, 'ravaged' is not too strong a word; the doocot filled a similar role to today's deep freeze and few doocots held under 500 pairs of birds. It has been calculated that two pigeons eat four bushels of corn a year.

In France the doocot came under the guillotine in 1789 but in Britain, more prosaically, it was the turnip which made it obsolete because its introduction from Sweden in the eighteenth century rendered the doocot a thing of the past. The farmer then had food with which to overwinter his beasts instead of slaughtering them in the autumn and salting their meat for winter providence.

It is a pity that pigeons have almost disappeared from the menu but the march

Hamilton House, built in 1628, Prestonpans.

of history and economics on gastronomy is inexorable. So from Edinburgh and the south-west we go out on a whirring fantasy of pigeons, a glamorous sight today but one that down the centuries the millers of Preston Mill and elsewhere cannot have welcomed.

11

ENVOI

ALTHOUGH SCOTLAND is one of the smaller countries of Europe, it has a longer coastline than the continent's largest country west of the Soviet Union, France. This shoreline has made the Scots as a nation at once outgoing in their, sometimes forced, travels and receptive to the influence of incomers and ideas from beyond the British Isles whether they came with invaders or guests.

Having been for centuries one of the poorer countries of the Western civilisation, it could have been expected that the artefacts it has to offer might be as scarce as money and meal has sometimes been in the rugged northern half of Britain, but Scotland's native genius and its contacts with the outside world have ensured that this is not at all the case. For although Scotland has never been rich or powerful in an international sense, neither has it ever been totally subjugated to a foreign power. Its small population, even today under five and a half million people, has given it space in which to allow relics and old buildings to be venerated and preserved and places of natural beauty in the mountains, islands and glens to stay undesecrated by industry and other 'development'.

The Scots also have a strong sense of their own identity and well-forged links with their past. In an increasingly internationally conformist society these are valuable assets for conservationists, because such individualism naturally treasures the hallmarks of the separateness of its origins. So it is not difficult in Scotland to arouse support for preserving a site or a building which reflects the country's history or is typical of a sentimentally remembered way of life. There are strongly protective lobbies for keeping remote Highland glens and bens untrammelled by access roads and touristic developments and leaving them empty for people who are prepared to walk and climb and live with the countryside as it is, instead of having it ameliorated for them to suit the urban softness of their lives.

The National Trust for Scotland has taken full advantage of such sentiments in gaining and maintaining support for the properties which it owns and manages throughout the country. It has done so successfully for the most part because its aims command wide public acclaim and because of the dedication and hard work of its staff and its many volunteer supporters. Also because owners of desirable properties, be they buildings, gardens, islands or tracts of land worthy of preservation have been quick to recognise in the Trust and the bodies with which it is associated like the Countryside Commission, the Scottish Wildlife Trust, the Historic Buildings Council, the Scottish Development Department and the Nature Conservancy Council, the best chance of preserving what could otherwise easily be lost or overwhelmed.

It is quite comforting to know that there are still apostles of this kind of conservatism around, the kind epitomised by the Cavalier soldier, statesman and poet, Lucius Carey, Viscount Falkland, who gave the motto to conservative philosophy: 'When it is not necessary to change, it is necessary not to change', much admired by Buchan and quoted by him in his masterly biography of Montrose.

Falkland died at the Battle of Newbury in 1643 and it is not without a certain irony that his most celebrated published work is called *Discources of Infallibility*, but historical allusion, however entertaining, need not falsify his dogma. In fact it exemplifies the dilemma and the struggle which the National Trust for Scotland constantly has to face. To what degree is preservation an imperative and is it always derogatory to adapt a site of historical, architectural or aesthetic interest to a modern use?

Adaptation can mean that the privileges and pleasures of the property can be enjoyed by more people at many different levels of appreciation. The museum principle cannot always be the guiding factor and, at times, can prove positively obstructive to the common good. A fine line has to be drawn between the wishes of the conservationists — almost always people with a strong historical focus and enthusiasts for a particular aspect of non-change whether the bias is architectural, historical, archaeological or towards preservation of wild places like mountains or islands — and public use and access. Privileged wildernesses, whether they be unoccupied buildings or mountain tops, are alien to the social philosophies of our time.

The National Trust for Scotland has patrolled this dangerous frontier well and with considerable awareness and discretion, and its work has made available to hundreds of thousands of people areas of Scotland, its treasures in buildings and landscapes, gardens, islands and historical sites which would not have been accessible but for the Trust's enlightened approaches to the problems entailed.

To hold in trust a significant part of the nation's history and identity is no small achievement.